The

BRITISH
MOTORWAYS

WHERE TO EAT, WHAT TO SEE
AND WHERE TO STAY CLOSE BY
THE MOTORWAY

Leslie and Adrian Gardiner

Illustrations by Elly King

PELHAM BOOKS

Key/Zeichenerklarung/Legends

H
Hotel, motel or guesthouse
Hotel, Motel oder Gasthaus
Hôtel, motel ou pension de famille

Park, garden, farm, zoo or place of natural beauty
Park, Garten, Bauernhof, Zoo oder Naturschauplatz
Parc, jardin public, ferme, zoo ou site pittoresque

IOI
Place to eat
Restaurationsbetrieb
Lieu de restauration

Museum or art gallery
Museum oder Kunstgalerie
Musée ou galerie

Stately home, castle, or building of architectural or historic interest
Herrschaftshaus, Burg, Schloss oder architektonisch/historisch
  interressantes Gebäude oder Bauwerk
Manoir historique, château ou batiment présentant un intérêt architectural
  ou historique

Cathedral, abbey, church or other place of worship
Dom, Abtei, Kirche oder anderes Andachtsstätte
Cathédrale, abbaye, église ou autre lieu de culte

Place of general interest
Allgemeine Sehenswürdigkeit
Lieu présentant un intérêt général

First published in Great Britain by
Pelham Books Ltd
27 Wrights Lane
London W8 5TZ
1987

This book was designed and produced b
The Festival Press Limited
5 Dryden Street
London WC2E 9NW

British Library Cataloguing in Publication Data

Gardiner, Leslie
    Best of British motorways.
    1. Automobiles — Road guides — Great Britain 2.
    Great Britain — Description and travel — 1971 —
    Guide-books I. Title
    914.1′04858   GV1025.G7

ISBN 0-7207-1741-8

Typesetting by Fleetsword, London.
Origination by Hong Kong Graphic Arts.
Printed by G. Canale and Co. Turin, Italy.

This book is a guide to places of interest. Diagrammatic motorway maps are included to help travellers find the destinations they wish to visit. The book is not intended for use as a motorway atlas. Information contained herein is correct at the time of going to press, but because roads, opening times and telephone numbers can alter no responsibility can be accepted by the publisher or copyright holder for such alterations.

The Festival Press Limited would like to thank the following people for their contributions to this book: Roger Boffey, map artist; David Heidenstam, editor; Susan Kinsey, additional illustrations.

Contents

M1: London to Leeds, 191m (306km), including M10, The St Albans spur, 4m (6.5km)

The M1 begins in north London and takes a fairly direct path to the industrial cities of West Yorkshire. For most of its route it manages to avoid large towns, and the traveller is hardly aware of passing within a few minutes' drive of Luton, Northampton, Leicester, Nottingham, Sheffield and other densely-populated places.

The motorway opens up a countryside which was relatively unknown to those who used to follow the traditional long-distance highways radiating from the capital. A quiet land of slow-flowing rivers is succeeded by the hunting and agricultural scenery of the Shires, then the district of once-vast estates known as the Dukeries. But hereabouts the effects of the coal-mining, ancient and modern, on which much of that rural wealth was founded, begin to be seen on either side; and north of Junction 32 (link with the M18), the route traverses country of increasingly industrial character.

Just before it reaches Leeds, the M1 crosses the M62. The M1 terminus a few miles farther on is also the terminus of the M621 Leeds spur, by which one might return to the M62 and the M1 southbound, and do the whole trip again in the other direction without changing gear. Included in this description is the M10, a short spur from Junction 7 to St Albans.

JUNCTION 1

2m (3km) S on Golders Green Road

Hampstead Heath
Notable oasis of greenery with walks and picnic spots; bathing, kite-flying, model-yachting, bank holiday fairs. Among fine houses discreetly sited is **Kenwood House,** N side of Heath; Adam library, good paintings, summer concerts beside the lake. At 20 Maresfield Gardens, Hampstead,

new **Sigmund Freud Museum,** where founder of psychoanalysis lived and worked; 'anyone missing this needs their head examined', says publicity.

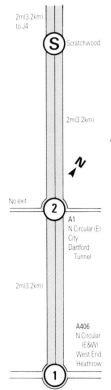

2m(3.2km) to J4

S Scratchwood

2m(3.2km)

N

No exit

2 A1
N Circular (E)
City
Dartford
Tunnel

2m(3.2km)

A406
N Circular
(E&W)
West End
Heathrow

1

JUNCTION 2

1m (1.5km) W on Grahame Park Way

Royal Air Force Museums, Hendon. A group of 'official' museums on site of pioneer flying training school, incorporating Royal Air Force Museum (150 machines from Blériot's biplane to the latest jump-jet); Battle of Britain Museum (aircraft native and foreign, radar, searchlights, barrage balloons); and Bomber Command Museum (almost every kind of World War II bomber, including extinct specimens); library, restaurant, shop; spick and span and carries faint air of unreality.

JUNCTION 5

3m (5km) SE (signposted)
Aldenham Country Park Pleasant landscaped area of meadow, woodland and open water; lakeside paths, fishing, adventure playground; pets' corner; grazing cattle.

3m (4.5km) SW off Nascot Wood Road, Watford
Cheslyn Gardens A carefully-organized area of ornamental garden, shrubbery, herbaceous plants, rock and woodland gardens; newly-established aviary, breeding birds; horticultural demonstrations.

2m (3km) SW on Watford Bypass
Spiders Web motel Low-built, modern but not flashy, superior rooms and a restaurant and salad bar. Tel: (01) 950 6211.

JUNCTION 6
4m (6.5km) NE on A405
St Albans See Junction 7

JUNCTION 7
ST ALBANS

4m (6.5km) E on M10

Important Roman city (Verulamium); brick-built **cathedral,**

originally a Norman Benedictine abbey, has longest nave in Europe;

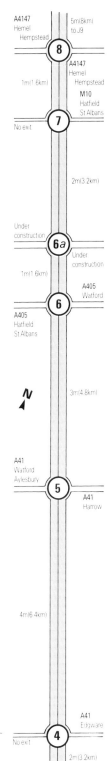

Roman wall along The Causeway in public park; **Roman theatre** and hypocaust; 15th-century **curfew tower; French Row,** narrow street of little trades; **Musical Museum,** Camp Road, has all kinds of mechanical instruments (some played on Suns.). 2m (3km) S at Chiswell

Green, **Gardens of the Rose,** showground of Royal National Rose Society, closed in winter; **Sally Lunn's Eating House,** 17 St Michael's Street; renowned ancient hostelry, now a superior oak-beamed restaurant. Tel: (0727) 54405.

JUNCTION 8

4m (6.5km) NW on B486
Piccotts End Upper and lower rooms of cottage have important wall paintings, probably 15th-century, discovered in 1953, portraying New Testament subjects; also priest's hole, ancient well and relics of building's 19th-century use as the very first cottage hospital; closed Jan., Feb.

6m (9.5km) W on A41

Berkhamsted Castle Extensive ruins of large motte-and-bailey Saxon fortress where Saxon leaders submitted to William the Conqueror (1066).

M1: *9-11*

JUNCTION 9

🌳 🏛️

7m (11km) W off A5
Whipsnade Biggest open zoo in Britain and the first of its kind; 18,000 animals, some of which cooperate in innocent performances.

7m (11km) E via leafy lanes, unclassified

Shaw's Corner, Ayot St Lawrence. Home of G.B. Shaw 1906-1950; just as he left it. Closed Fri., Sat.

JUNCTION 10

🏰 🌳 🏛️ H 🍴

1m (1.5km) E off A1081

Luton Hoo Majestic Adam house and Capability Brown park; old masters, tapestries, ivories, and Fabergé objects. Closed in winter.

3m (5km) N on A1081
Luton Museum, Wardown Park, Luton. Story of town's famous straw-hat industry; also lace-making down the ages, another Luton speciality; all housed in a fine Victorian mansion in parkland.

4m (7km) SE on A1081
Milton Hotel, 25 Milton Road, Harpenden. Neat, unpretentious set-up, good décor in bedrooms; satisfying but fairly plain fare; moderate. Tel: (058 27) 62914.

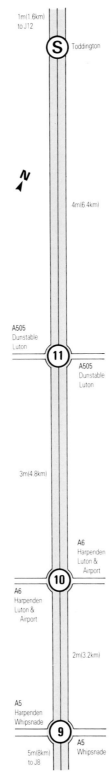

1m(1.6km) to J12

Ⓢ Toddington

N

4m(6.4km)

A505 Dunstable Luton

⑪

A505 Dunstable Luton

3m(4.8km)

A6 Harpenden Luton & Airport

⑩

A6 Harpenden Luton & Airport

2m(3.2km)

A5 Harpenden Whipsnade

⑨

A5 Whipsnade

5m(8km) to J8

JUNCTION 11

🌳 📷

3m (5km) E on A505
Luton Museum See Junction 10

7m (12km) SW off B489
Whipsnade See Junction 9

8m (13km) SW off B489
Ivinghoe Beacon Splendid viewpoint on Chilterns ridge; G.K. Chesterton, fumbling in his pocket for a stick of chalk, realized he was sitting on the biggest stick of chalk in the world. Close at hand, historic Pitstone **Wind and Water Mills** (National Trust); also picnic places with views of gliding from Dunstable Downs. 2m (3km) N of Beacon, off A4146, **Edlesborough Craft Centre,** Slicketts Lane, Edlesborough, family-run craft centre, keenly-priced gifts.

10m (16km) NW on A5, then signposted at Hockliffe

Leighton Buzzard Narrow Gauge Railway, Page's Park. Tiny-gauge line (2ft (60cm)) runs 5½m (9km) on wavering and hilly route; comical little locomotives; special appeal for children. Operates Sun. and public holidays, also Wed. in high season; closed in winter.

4½m (7km) NW on A5130

Woburn Abbey,
Woburn. Last word in
mass-entertainment
stately homes;
widespread classical
palace (Marquess of
Tavistock), stable
blocks, outbuildings in
40 acres (16 hectares) of
gardens and pleasure
grounds; garden centre,
camping exhibition;
antiques centre; world-
renowned artists
represented in paintings
collection; porcelain
(Sèvres) and silver (Paul
Lamerie); in park,
Woburn Wild Animal
Kingdom, drive-through
safari park; sky ride
above the animals;
boating, ghost train and
much more. House
closed weekdays in
winter.

4m (6.5km) N on A5120
Flitwick Manor hotel,
Flitton. Restaurant is
above average; seafood
a specialty; not
expensive. Tel: (0525)
712242.

JUNCTION 13

5m (8km) S on A5130
Woburn Abbey See
Junction 12

*10m (16km) S via Woburn,
signposted from A5*
**Leighton Buzzard
Narrow Gauge Railway**
See Junction 11

8m (13km) N off A421
Moot Hall, Elstow. John
Bunyan memorabilia in
15th-century market hall
of his native village.

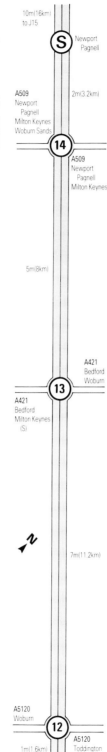

10m(16km)
to J15

S Newport
Pagnell

A509
Newport
Pagnell
Milton Keynes
Woburn Sands

2m(3.2km)

14

A509
Newport
Pagnell
Milton Keynes

5m(8km)

A421
Bedford
Woburn

13

A421
Bedford
Milton Keynes
(S)

7m(11.2km)

A5120
Woburn

12

A5120
Toddington

1m(1.6km)
to services

*1½m (2.5km) W off Childs
Way, Milton Keynes*

Peace Pagoda Exotic
Japanese Buddhist
monument dedicated to
world peace; first in
western hemisphere; in
attractive parkland
round Willen lake;
picnics, boating, fishing.

*5m (8km) W off A5 near
Stony Stratford*
Ouse Valley Park
Various quiet
unspectacular walks
along meandering Ouse
river; at Old Wolverton
the **Iron Trunk
aqueduct,** early
19th-century.

*5m (8km) S near A5 and
Fenny Stratford railway
station*
Fenny Lodge Gallery
Paintings, embroideries,
pots, sculptures, glass
and jewelry in a solid
Georgian canalside
house. Closed Sun.

13m (21km) W on A422
Movie Museum, Market
Hill, Buckingham.
Home movie nostalgia;
vintage ciné-cameras
bought and sold; old
films shown; while film
buffs remain enthralled,
others may enjoy
strolling round the tiny
market township.

JUNCTION 15

2m (3km) NE on A508

Musical Merry-go-Round, Wootton. Magnificent old-time fairground carousel and valuable assembly of Wurlitzers employed in musical shows; dancing; occasional 'sight and sound' spectaculars; a great and unique experience.

4m (6.5km) NE on A508

Museum of Leathercraft, Bridge Street, Northampton. History of local industry, predominantly footwear, from early days. Closed Sun.

7m (11km) NE on A508 and A45
Billing Aquadrome
Leisure complex in well-watered parkland on River Nene; 9 lakes; play areas; miniature train; much patronized by caravanners.

3m (5km) S on A508

Waterways Museum, Stoke Bruerne. On banks of Grand Union Canal and close to Blisworth canal tunnel, longest still in commercial use;

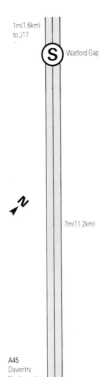

1m(1.6km) to J17

(S) Watford Gap

7m(11.2km)

A45 Daventry Northampton (W)

16

A45 Northampton (W) Oxford (A43)

4m(6.4km)

Rothersthorpe (S)

3m(4.8km)

A508 Northampton Milton Keynes (N)

15

A508 Northampton

10m(16km) to services

excellent display of dress, cabin furnishings, prints and photographs evocative of 2 centuries of working boatmen's and boatwomen's lives. Closed Mon. in winter.

JUNCTION 16

5m (8km) E on A45
Alternative access to **Billing Aquadrome** and **Leathercraft Museum,** Northampton. See Junction 15

6m (9.5km) N off A45, skirting Northampton
Althorp Early Georgian mansion of dignity and character (Earl Spencer, father of Princess of Wales); rich storehouse of paintings, porcelain, furniture; fine grounds, but visitors strictly regimented; special 'connoisseurs' tours' on Weds.

JUNCTION 18

7m (11km) E off A428
Coton Manor Gardens, Ravensthorpe. Long years of unremitting toil have produced these outstanding country gardens; terraces, old hedges and lawns;

flamingoes, cranes; rare and unusual plants sold at nursery. Open Thur., Sun. and sometimes Wed., summer only.

9m (14.5km) E on A50
Guilsborough Grange Wildlife Park A popular park exhibiting a variety of birds and beasts; country stroll (15 mins) among wild flowers; resident falconer gives demonstrations.

12m (19km) NE on B4036
Purlieu Farm, Naseby. A museum dealing with old-time agricultural life and the battle of Naseby (1645); closed in winter.

5m (8km) W on A428

Rugby School Scene of *Tom Brown's Schooldays* and of invention of oval-ball football game; chapel and close are visitable.

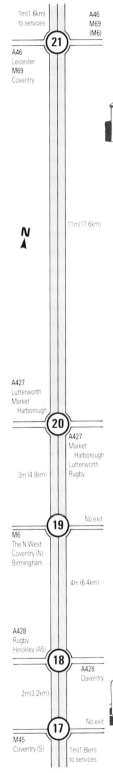

1m(1.6km) to services

A46 M69 (M6)

21

A46 Leicester M69 Coventry

N

11m(17.6km)

A427 Lutterworth Market Harborough

20

A427 Market Harborough Lutterworth Rugby

3m (4.8km)

No exit

19

M6 The N West Coventry (N) Birmingham

4m (6.4km)

A428 Rugby Hinckley (A5)

18

A428 Daventry

2m(3.2km)

No exit

17

M45 Coventry (S)

1m(1.6km) to services

JUNCTION 20

3m (5km) SE via Lutterworth on B5414

Stanford Hall Late 17th-century house; pictures include a valuable collection of Stuart portraits; fine 13th-century church; replica of flying machine (motorized glider) in which pioneer aeronaut Percy Pilcher was killed in this park, 1899, in what might have been the world's first powered flight. **Stanford Museum,** a select and constantly-changing exhibition of rare motor-cycles and three-wheelers.

JUNCTION 21

LEICESTER
5m (8km) NE on A46
A busy city with slow-moving traffic at all times. Worth seeing are **Cathedral Jewry Wall Museum, Archaeological Museum** and **Wygston's House** (museum of fashion, with old-time drapers' and shoe shops), all at St Nicholas Circle; and **Newarke Houses,** The Newarke, reconstructed Jacobean street scene.

On W outskirts, off B5380 (recrossing motorway), **Kirby Muxloe,** dramatic ruin

of large fortified and moated medieval house.

JUNCTION 22

8m (13km) E on A50
Leicester See
Junction 21

9m (14.5km) SW via B585

Bosworth Battlefield,
near Market Bosworth.
Country park and visitor
centre with historical
mock-ups, tombs and
solemn music; arms and
armour; battlefield
trails; periodical
pageantry
commemorates
Plantagenet-Tudor
rivalry and re-enacts
battle of 1485, decisive
in English history.
Closed in winter.

8m (13km) SW on A447
Cadeby, near Market
Bosworth. Major brass-
rubbing centre, with
instruction in this far-
from-trivial pursuit. In
rectory gardens, **Cadeby
Light Railway,** very
light indeed; runs on
2nd Sat. of month.

JUNCTION 23

3m (5km) E on A512
Great Central Railway,
Central Station, S
Loughborough. Steam
trains with luxury and
wine/dine services on
5m (8km) route
Loughborough-Rothley
through pleasant
Charnwood Forest
scenery; 16 historic
locomotives; picnic
opportunities; Sat. and
Sun. all year, also Wed.
from June to Sept.

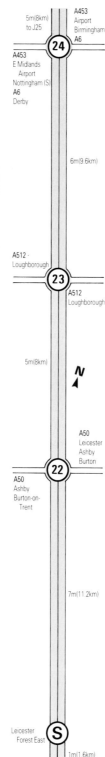

5m(8km)
to J25

A453
Airport
Birmingham
A6

(24)

A453
E Midlands
Airport
Nottingham (S)
A6
Derby

6m(9.6km)

A512 ·
Loughborough

(23)

A512
Loughborough

5m(8km)

N

A50
Leicester
Ashby
Burton

(22)

A50
Ashby
Burton-on-
Trent

7m(11.2km)

Leicester
Forest East

(S)

1m(1.6km)
to J21

JUNCTION 24

4m (6.5km) W on A453

**Donington Racing Car
Collection,** Castle
Donington.
Meticulously displayed,
a fleet of single-seater
racing cars from 1930s
onwards in
museum at race-track
entrance recalls years
when Donington Park
was a major road-racing
ciruit, associated with
past champions like
Nuvolari, Caracciola;
also racing motor-cycles;
short on archive
material; expensive
entrance charge. Closed
Christmas week.

*11m (17.5km) SW off
A453*

Staunton Harold Hall,
near Calke.
'Unsurpassed for its
complete Englishness',
says Nicholas Pevsner;
Saxon foundation,
Jacobean with Palladian
trimmings, the place is
better value than
grandiose and much-
publicized **Calke Abbey**
down the road; broad
lake and thick
woodland; the little
church, being
Cromwellian, is a rarity.
Open Wed.-Sun.,
Apr.-Oct.

JUNCTION 25

*3m (5km) NW on byroads
via Stanton by Dale*
Dale Abbey Only 1 arch
of ancient abbey
survives, but in rockface
there is a one-time
hermit's cell and cave;
½m (1km) N of abbey,

**Cat and Fiddle
windmill.**

NOTTINGHAM

8m (13km) E on A52
Sprawling metropolis of
tobacco, lace and
bicycles.

Castle Museum,
good silver
and ceramics,
landscapes by
Nottingham-born
Bonington and Paul
Sandby, Sherwood
Foresters regimental
relics; **Green's Mill,**
Sneinton Dale, working
windmill and portrayal
of 19th-century wind-
power technology;
Costume Museum,
Castle Gate; **Industrial
Museum,** Wollaton
Park, explaining history
of lace, tobacco and
pharmaceutical
industries; and **Lace
Centre,** Castle Road,
housed in an historic
building and telling
story of lace-making in
Nottingham, illustrated
with antique machinery
and beautiful lace-

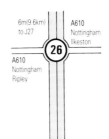

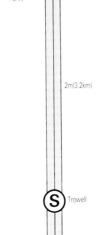

6m(9.6km)
to J27

A610
Nottingham
Ilkeston

26

A610
Nottingham
Ripley

2m(3.2km)

S Trowell

4m(6.4km)

A52
Nottingham
Derby
Ilkeston

25

A52
Nottingham
Derby

5m(8km)
to J24

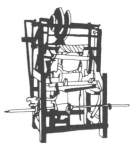

covered panels. **William
Booth Walkabout**
(leaflet at tourist office)
embraces scenes of life
and work of Salvation
Army founder.
Nottingham Caves,
Bridlesmith Gate, offer
subterranean walking
tour of medieval
domestic and
commercial caverns. **La
Grenouille restaurant,**
Lenton Boulevard;
bistro atmosphere, wide
choice, chiefly French
dishes; moderately
priced. Tel: (0602)
411088. 2m (3km) E of
city at Holme Pierrepont
(A52) is **National
Watersports Centre;**
continuous summer
programmes of sailing,
canoeing, windsurfing,
water-skiing, special
aquatic displays;
waterbus service from
Trent Bridge, Sat. and
Sun. in summer.

JUNCTION 26

5m (8km) SE on A610
Nottingham See
Junction 25

5m (8km) NW on A610
**D.H. Lawrence
Birthplace Museum,**
Victoria Street,
Eastwood. Furnished to
the period, with
appropriate
Lawrentiana; leaflets
available, showing
scenes of novels within
walking distance;
rentable holiday
apartments at **The
Breach,** Garden Road,
the Lawrence family
home, mentioned in
Sons and Lovers.

11

M1: *27-30*

JUNCTION 27

4m (6.5km) E on A611 and B683

Newstead Abbey
Childhood home of
Lord Byron; some of the
poet's personal
belongings on show;
700-year-old Gospel Oak
at main gates; beautiful
but somewhat
melancholy parkland,
ponds, waterfalls; rock
and water gardens.
Closed in winter.

4m (6.5km) SW on A608
**D.H. Lawrence
Birthplace Museum** See
Junction 26

JUNCTION 28

10m (16km) W off A6

**National Tramway
Museum,** Crich. Open-
air tracks loaded with
trams old and new from
Britain and abroad; a
colourful scene; rides
offered on woodland
route above Derwent
valley; horsedrawn
trams; closed Fri. and all
winter.

*15m (24km) NE on A615
and A6075 near
Edwinstowe*
Sherwood Forest Area is
large, agricultural,
partly built over, but
unspoiled tracts survive

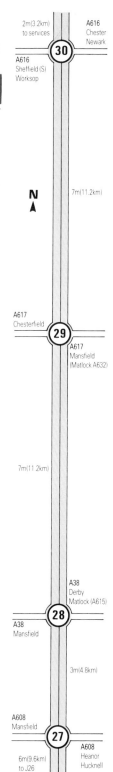

around Edwinstowe;
Visitor Centre,
Edwinstowe, on B6034;
ranger service;
waymarked paths to
Major Oak and other
features of Sherwood
lore; **Robin Hood's
Larder** serves snacks;
Edwinstowe **church** said
to be where real Robin
Hood was married.

JUNCTION 29

4m (6.5km) NE on A632
Bolsover Castle Lordly
structure on hilltop;
home of 16th-century
Bess of Hardwick
(Elizabeth, Countess of
Shrewsbury); **Little
Castle** offshoot is a
charming folly.

3m (5km) SE off A617
Hardwick Hall 'More
glass than wall' —
another lofty pile by
'Building Bess',
remarkable for size and
number of its windows;
large herb garden;
nature trail; closed
Mon., Tue. and all
winter.

JUNCTION 30

4m (6.5km) E on A616
Creswell Crags Narrow
limestone gorge with
caves of prehistoric
creatures; visitor centre
has exhibition and
audio-visuals; pathway
to gorge and lake; picnic
site.

JUNCTION 31

3m (5km) SW off A618

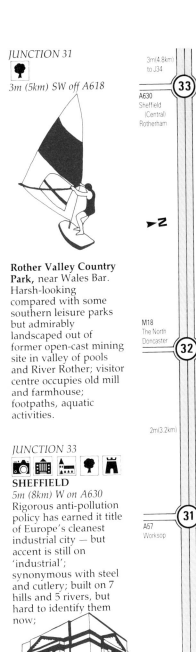

Rother Valley Country Park, near Wales Bar. Harsh-looking compared with some southern leisure parks but admirably landscaped out of former open-cast mining site in valley of pools and River Rother; visitor centre occupies old mill and farmhouse; footpaths, aquatic activities.

JUNCTION 33

SHEFFIELD

5m (8km) W on A630
Rigorous anti-pollution policy has earned it title of Europe's cleanest industrial city — but accent is still on 'industrial'; synonymous with steel and cutlery; built on 7 hills and 5 rivers, but hard to identify them now;

City Museum in Weston Park near university holds definitive collection of Sheffield plate; the **Mappin,** also Weston Park, and **Graves,** Surrey Street, are first-class art galleries;

medieval **cathedral** in Church Street has acquired glass-and-steel doors and an ultra-modern annexe;

Industrial Museum on artificial Kelham Island off Alma Street covers city's working history from huge steam engines to delicate craft workshops; famous contemporary theatre, the **Crucible,** has excellent inexpensive restaurant and coffee bar; busy night life, many discos; **Round Walk** of 10m (16km) goes entirely through city parks on S of centre, with splendid panoramas of Derbyshire hills.

ROTHERHAM

3m (4.5km) N on A618
Two-storey, square, 18th-century folly,

Boston Castle, off Moorgate Road; erected by local nobleman who supported American colonists' action at 'Boston Tea Party' (1774); from surrounding park, wide views of Rother valley and hills; in Clifton Park, **Clifton House Museum,** noted for its distinguished collection of Rockingham china.

M1: 34-38

2m(3.2km)
to J39

JUNCTION 34
2½m (4km) SW on A6109
Sheffield See
Junction 33

3m (5km) NE on A6109
Rotherham See
Junction 33

JUNCTION 35

WENTWORTH
2m (3km) NE on B6090
In village, a **craft
workshop complex**
produces extensive
range of hand-made
articles. Short distance
E, **Wentworth
Woodhouse**,
monumental Georgian
palace with longest
facade of any building in
England, now a teacher-
training college but
woodland paths open to
public — along them,
monoliths of **Hoober
Stand, Needle's Eye**

and **Keppel's Column**,
all commemorative of
events in unconvention-
al lives of Marquesses of
Rockingham.

JUNCTION 36

2½m (4km) W off A629
Wortley Top Forge
Water-driven iron forge,
300 years old, said to be
unique; dams, sluices,
waterwheels, hammers;
under restoration but
open to inspection.

2½m (4km) NE on A61
**Worsborough Country
Park** Low-key dell and
stream, conservation
project, gamely
struggling against grim
surroundings; star
attraction is 17th-
century water-driven
corn mill, now working
again.

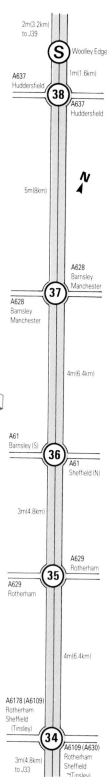

S — Woolley Edge
1m(1.6km)

A637
Huddersfield
38
A637
Huddersfield

N

5m(8km)

A628
Barnsley
Manchester
37
A628
Barnsley
Manchester

4m(6.4km)

A61
Barnsley (S)
36
A61
Sheffield (N)

3m(4.8km)

A629
Rotherham
35
A629
Rotherham

4m(6.4km)

A6178 (A6109)
Rotherham
Sheffield
(Tinsley)
34
A6109 (A630)
Rotherham
Sheffield
(Tinsley)
3m(4.8km)
to J33

JUNCTION 37

*4m (6.5km) NW on A628
and A635*
Cannon Hall,
Cawthorne. Georgian
house, now **museum** of
period-furnished rooms
containing, among other
things, the National
Loan collection of Dutch
and Flemish paintings
(Harvey Bequest) and
regimental relics of
13th/18th Hussars, not
to mention the bow of
Little John of outlaw
fame; former estate is a
country park.
Cawthorne, 1m (1.5km)
S, is a surprisingly
pretty village.

JUNCTION 38

1½m (2.5km) W on A637

**Yorkshire Sculpture
Park**, Bretton Hall, West
Bretton. Sounds a
grandiloquent note, but
is impressive enough
with lawns and
woodland dotted with
sculptures in various
media, serious and
comic, by the famous
and not-yet-famous;
administrative district of
Wakefield, whose
council controls Bretton
Hall, embraces
birthplaces of Henry
Moore and Barbara
Hepworth, premier
British sculptors, both
represented by works in
Park; periodical
exhibitions, summer
workshops, artistic
events.

JUNCTION 39

1½m (2.5km) E on B6378

Sandal Castle, Sandal
Magna. Some
imagination called for,
to dress these fragments
in the turrets and
crenellations of Richard
III's favourite northern
stronghold; impressive
arches of 14th-century
St Helen's church, close
by, have more
successfully resisted the
'stealing hand of Time'.

*7m (11km) E on B6378
and A638*
Nostell Priory See M62,
Junction 32

¼m (0.5km) W on A636

Cedar Court hotel,
Calder Grove.
Caravanserai of
refinement in a
gastronomic desert, and
close to motorway
junction; modern style;
100 neat and uncluttered
rooms offering all
amenities; 2 restaurants,
of which *La Tour
d'Argent* has authentic
continental cuisine and
a tempting wine list;
expensive by local
standards. Tel: (0924)
276310.

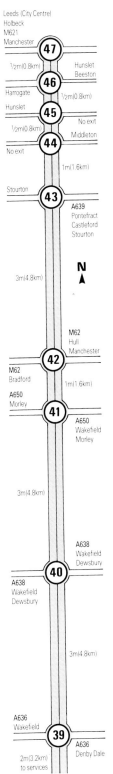

Leeds (City Centre)
Holbeck
M621
Manchester
47

½m(0.8km) — Hunslet / Beeston
46

Harrogate
Hunslet — ½m(0.8km)
45 — No exit

½m(0.8km) — Middleton
44
No exit

1m(1.6km)

Stourton
43
A639
Pontefract
Castleford
Stourton

3m(4.8km)

N

M62
Hull
Manchester
42

M62
Bradford — 1m(1.6km)

A650
Morley
41
A650
Wakefield
Morley

3m(4.8km)

A638
Wakefield
Dewsbury
40
A638
Wakefield
Dewsbury

3m(4.8km)

A636
Wakefield
39
A636
Denby Dale

2m(3.2km)
to services

JUNCTION 40
*5m (8km) NW on A638
and A652*
**Oakwell Hall Country
Park** See M62
Junction 27

JUNCTION 43
*4½m (7km) NE off
A63/A642, signposted*
Temple Newsam See
M62 Junction 30

JUNCTION 44
*2m (3km) W on Tunstall
Road*
Middleton Railway See
M62 Junction 28

JUNCTION 47
M1 meets M621
Access to central **Leeds,**
1m (1.5km) See M621,
Junctions 2 and 3

M11:
London to Girton, 54m (86km)

A102(M): Greenwich to Blackwall Tunnel, 1½m (2.5km), and Bow to Hackney, 1½m (2.5km)

Essex is sometimes thought of as a dull county, but the M11, along its western boundaries, sweeps across an undulating landscape of prosperous farms and villages, many of the former looking like heritage properties, many of the latter contending for a 'prettiest village' title. In these regions the past is always whispering in one's ear, for they were among the earliest inhabited parts of England. The mellow brick and half-timbering of the architecture summarize just what foreign visitors think of when they visualize rural England.

The northern part of the route forms a partial bypass for Cambridge, which is itself the centre of a quiet district, flat and reedy and full of historical interest. The short spur which leaves the M11 at Junction 9, going north-east to Stump Cross (2m (3km)), is the beginning of a projected motorway to Newmarket and Norwich, deeper into the land of fens and broads. But at present the M11 is East Anglia's only motorway, and normally peaceful.

Access from Kent to the present beginning of the M11 (Junction 3) is facilitated by two short stretches of M-type highway through the East End of London. One is south of the river in Greenwich, the other north of the river at Bow; both are numbered A102(M).

JUNCTION 3

5m (8km) S on A117
Old Station Museum, Pier Road, North Woolwich. Reconstructed Great Eastern Railway station (c. 1910) with many relics including locomotives; short distance upstream, view

of **Thames Flood Barrier,** extra-terrestrial-looking structure spanning Thames; huge shining cowls of shipping gates pivot to cope with high incoming tides; visitor centre on S shore, via Woolwich ferry.

JUNCTION 4
1m (1.5km) W on A406
Start of **Epping Forest Trail** See Junction 5

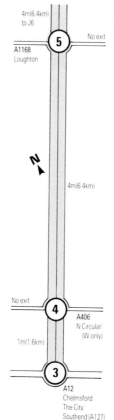

4m(6.4km) to J6

5

No exit

A1168
Loughton

N

4m(6.4km)

No exit

4

A406
N Circular
(W only)

1m(1.6km)

3

A12
Chelmsford
The City
Southend (A127)
Dartford Tunnel

JUNCTION 5

2½m (4km) W via Loughton on A1168

Epping Forest
Noteworthy and very popular area; **museum** of forest history and **hunting lodge** of Queen Elizabeth I; at Chingford, S end of Forest middle of Forest at A11/A121 intersection, **Essex Way,** long-distance footpath begins; also **Forest Way** to Hatfield Forest near Bishop's Stortford, a 22m (35km) walk; at **High Beach,** Waltham Abbey, conservation centre with 2 pre-Roman earthworks.

JUNCTION 7

2m (3km) W off B1393
Parndon Wood Nature reserve on S outskirts of Harlow New Town.

5m (8km) W off A414

Rye House, off Stanstead Road, near Hoddesdon town centre. Fine sample of 15th-century brickwork and 'barley-sugar' chimneys; permanent exhibition on site; open Sat., Sun. and bank holidays, summer only. S from Rye House runs riverine vale of **Lee Valley Leisure Park.**
See M25 Junction 25

7m (11km) SE off A414
St Andrew's log church, Greensted. The only surviving Saxon wooden church in Britain.

3m (5km) W on A414
Moat House Saddle Room restaurant, Southern Way, Harlow. Wood-beamed dining-room; international cuisine; inexpensive *table d'hôte. Tel: (0279) 22441.*

JUNCTION 8

1m (1.5km) W on A120
Castle Gardens, Bishop's Stortford. Lavish layout of terraced flowerbeds and walks.

4m (6.5km) NW on B1383
Stanstead Mountfichet Unique life-sized model

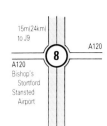

15m(24km) to J9

8

A120

A120 Bishop's Stortford Stansted Airport

N

10m(16km)

A414 Harlow

7

A414 Harlow Chelmsford

4m(6.4km)

M25 Dartford Tunnel (M20) Gatwick M23 Watford & M1 Heathrow Waltham Abbey

6

M25

4m(6.4km) to J5

---

of Norman motte-and-bailey castle with huts, palisades and watchtowers on site of feudal stronghold. Closed Dec.-Apr.

3½m (6km) SE off A120
Hatfield Forest National Trust preserves, lake and nature trails.

8m (13km) E on A120
Great Dunmow Famous since Chaucer's day for 'Dunmow Flitch', side of bacon awarded annually to a happily-married couple; otherwise an unpretentious little place of picturesque cottages; imposing 14th-century **St Mary's church,** noted for old stained glass.

11m (17.5km) NE via Bishop's Stortford and B1051, recrossing motorway.

THAXTED Possibly most attractive of country townships with white and colour-washed or half-timbered houses straggling down curve of hill; celebrated medieval **Guildhall** on timber pillars; nearby, sometime home of Gustav Holst the

composer. **John Webb's windmill** a landmark on hilltop.

M11: *9-11*

JUNCTION 9

SAFFRON WALDEN
6m (9.5km) SE via motorway spur and B1383

Market centre and social focus of several villages, all ancient with many historic buildings; in Saffron Walden the medieval street plan is complete; many fine Jacobean and Georgian houses on tree-lined slopes; **Sun Inn** (National Trust), lurching, deeply-gabled antique hostelry, has decorative carvings on facade and a maze in the garden; cathedral-like church of **St Mary the Virgin; museum.** *1m (1.5km) W of town,*

Audley End, stern Jacobean mansion of many little windows, 'improved' by Vanbrugh and Adam; Capability Brown park; one of England's great country houses; closed Mon. and all winter. **Eight Bells inn** and restaurant, Bridge Street, Saffron Walden; cheerful atmosphere, wide choice of bar-lunch dishes; inexpensive.

8m (13km) NE on A11, A604 and B1052 **Wildlife Breeding Centre,** Linton. Bears, leopards, bear-cats; educative park.

2m(3.2km) to J12 · A1309 Cambridge (S) A10 Royston

(11)

A1309 Cambridge (S) A10 Harston

5m(8km)

A505 Royston Duxford

(10)

A505 Colchester (A604) Saffron Walden Duxford

4m(6.4km)

(9) No exit

A11 Newmarket Norwich · 15m(24km) to J8

JUNCTION 10

1m (1.5km) W on A505

Imperial War Museum, Duxford. Spacious displays of military and civil aircraft, including Concorde; also miscellaneous war memorabilia; video of RAF Duxford history; passenger trips in 1930s aircraft; restaurant, picnic areas. Closed Nov.-Feb.

JUNCTION 11

3m (5km) E via Great Shelford, off A1307 **Gog and Magog Hills** Rural seclusion and panorama of Cambridge from modest altitude; at prehistoric **Wandlebury Ring,** picnicking, walking, nature area; near Ring, **grave of Godolphin,** Arab stallion who sired most English bloodstock, died 1753.

1½m (2.5km) N on A10 **'Hobson's Choice'** Fountain at junction of Lenfield and Trumpington roads commemorates Cambridge-London carter Thomas Hobson, afterwards a rich posthorse hirer, died 1630; he hired out his horses in strict rotation, hence the take-it-or-leave-it proverb.

JUNCTION 12

8m (13km) SW off A603
Wimpole Hall As pure
and well-proportioned
in style as any great
18th-century house;
folly and Chinese bridge
in park;

rare livestock
bred at thatched **Home
Farm;** agricultural
museum in Great Barn.
Children's play area;
lunch and tea at Hall;
picnic site. Closed
Mon., Fri. and all
winter.

*2m (3km) E on Fen
Causeway*
Coe Fen Marked trail in
meadowland beside the
Cam.

CAMBRIDGE
2½m (4km) NE on A603

Still a comparatively
tranquil city with much
greenery; multitudinous
bicycles emphasize
academic atmosphere
and constitute traffic
hazard. **Colleges,**
chiefly congregated
between parallel lines of
River Cam and main
thoroughfare, may be
visited by individuals
(no picnics, keep off
lawns, parties must take
official guide). A short
visit should embrace
The Backs, riverside

lawns, flowery in
spring; **Fitzwilliam
Museum** (closed Mon.);
**University Botanic
Gardens; Scott Polar
Research Institute**
(closed Sun.); new
**Museum of
Technology,** Cheddars
Lane; **Holy Sepulchre,**
one of four 'round'
churches left in
England; and **Kettles
Yard art gallery,** Castle
Street, for the best of
avant-garde painting
and sculpture by famous
and aspiring artists.

JUNCTION 13
2m (3km) E on A1303
Cambridge See
Junction 12

JUNCTION 14

*7m (11km) E on A45 and
B1102 near Lode*

Anglesey Abbey Typical
Jacobean house,
mullioned and gabled,
on site of ancient abbey;
admirable paintings and
ornaments; gardens
bristle with statuary;
working water-mill;
visitor centre. cafeteria,
shop. Closed Mon.,
Tue. and in winter.

*10m (16km) N on A604
and B1050*
Earith Here begin the
Vermuyden Cuts,
drainage channels to
The Wash with which
the 17th-century Dutch
engineer Vermuyden
dried out the weeping
bogs of Cambridgeshire;
village is tidal limit of
Old West River, which
from Earith back to its
source four counties
away is the Great Ouse.

Map labels (central strip):

No access
from A45(E)
or A1307

14

A45
Newmarket
(A10)
Ely
A604
The North
Huntingdon

N

2m(3.2km)

A1303
(A45W)
Bedford
Cambridge

13

No exit

2m(3.2km)

A603
Cambridge
Sandy

12

A603
Cambridge
Sandy

2m(3.2km)
to J11

M18:

Rotherham to Rawcliffe, 27m (43km)

The M18 is a cross-country motorway which enables traffic going north up the M1 or A1 to make for South Humberside and East Yorkshire. It leaves the M1 near Sheffield and proceeds via Doncaster to the head of the Humber estuary near Goole, where it links up with the M62. The route passes at first among towns of heavy industry but all the motorist sees are lovely rolling, wooded hills. Then comes a flat and agricultural countryside where outlying mining communities of the Yorkshire coalfields are scattered. The M18 is one of the quieter motorways.

JUNCTION 1
5m (8km) W on A631
Rotherham See M1
Junction 33

JUNCTION 3
2½m (4km) N on A6182
Doncaster See A1(M)
Junction C

JUNCTION 4
6m (9.5km) W on A630
Doncaster See A1(M)
Junction C

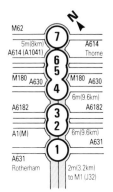

JUNCTION 6

1m (1.5km) E on A614
Belmont hotel, Horsefair Green, Thorne. A good inexpensive overnight or meal stop; 26 rooms; early dinner, but *à la carte* and substantial; good value bar meals and snacks. Tel: (0405) 812320.

M180:

Thorne to Melton Ross, 29m (46km) including M181 (Scunthorpe spur), 3m (5km)

The motorway leads east from the M18 towards Grimsby and comes to an end a few miles south of the Humber Bridge. The route is mainly agricultural. The eastern section crosses part of rural Lincolnshire within sight of the Wolds.

JUNCTION 1

HATFIELD
2m (3km) W on A18
Ancient village with beautiful little 12th-century church; gives name to Hatfield Chase, hunting forest and haunt of outlaws until Cornelius Vermuyden drained bogs and reclaimed land in 17th century.

JUNCTION 2

EPWORTH
4m (6.5km) S on A161
Village whose name Methodists conjure

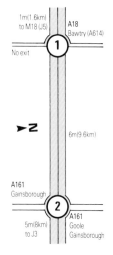

with; **Old Rectory** (visitable) was birthplace of John and Charles Wesley, evangelists; **Village Trail** embraces Rectory ('cradle of nonconformism') and other dignified buildings of Queen Anne style.

JUNCTION 3 (junction with M181)

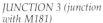

SCUNTHORPE

3m (5km) N on M181 and A18

Steel town not quite as black as painted; striped blinds and stalls of modern **Market Hall,** give Lincolnshire tradition a Continental twist; good **museum** in Oswald Road; green spacious **Central Park** off Ashby Road, with leisure centre and bistro;

famous old church of **St Lawrence's,** Frodingham; genuine Lincolnshire **windmill.**

6m (10km) N via Scunthorpe on B1430

Normanby Hall
Regency mansion in 350-acre (141-hectare) park; house noted for furniture and a costume collection; park has visitor trails; cafeteria, delightful picnic area. Closed Sat. in winter.

JUNCTION 4

KIRTON-IN-LINDSEY

5m (8km) N on A18 and (recrossing motorway) S off B1398

Local enthusiasts have assembled a **railway museum,** bric-à-brac collection, renovated **tower windmill** and **arts/crafts centre;** narrow-gauge **garden railway** under construction.

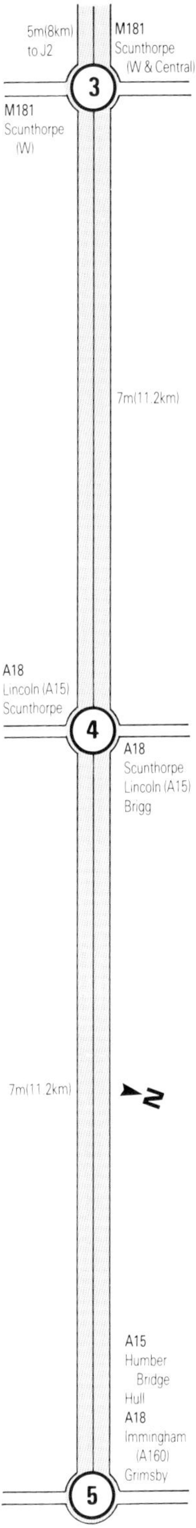

JUNCTION 5

9m (14.5km) off A180 and A1077 N

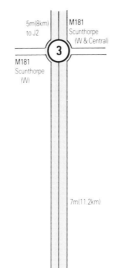

Thornton Abbey
Sizeable remains of 12th-century monastery with huge crenellated gatehouse; impressive ruin.

1m (1.5km) N of A15
Elsham Country Park
Lake, wildlife, rolling woodland in grounds of Elsham Hall; art gallery, forge, bird garden, adventure playground. Closed in winter except Sun. and bank holidays. **Granary Tea Room and Restaurant,** Elsham Park; home produce, inexpensive, in restored award-winning building.

1m (1.5km) SW on A18

Wrawby Postmill
Prominent landmark since 1760; exterior merits inspection; interior open bank holidays and occasional summer Sun. only. **Viking Way,** long-distance footpath south from Humber, crosses road hereabouts (look out for winged-helmet signs).

Map labels (centre column):

5m(8km) to J2

M181 Scunthorpe (W & Central)

3

M181 Scunthorpe (W)

7m(11.2km)

A18 Lincoln (A15) Scunthorpe

4

A18 Scunthorpe Lincoln (A15) Brigg

7m(11.2km)

A15 Humber Bridge Hull
A18 Immingham (A160) Grimsby

5

A1(M):

London to Tyneside

The A1(M) is at present far from complete. We describe the 3 fairly short sections — London to Baldock, Doncaster bypass and Scotch Corner to Tyneside — which have been raised to motorway standards. They are labelled A1(M) south, A1(M) central and A1(M) north.

A1(M) north:

Scotch Corner to Tyneside, 38m (61km), including A66(M) (Darlington) and A6127(M) (Newcastle-upon-Tyne)

Most northerly of the 3 motorway sections this route strides over the valleys of Tees and Wear and comes to rest near the banks of the Tyne, a short distance from the Tyne Tunnel. Junctions are numbered from the south — in brackets, because this route has not been allotted official junction numbers. The short divergence to Darlington, A66(M), has motorway status; as has the urban through-route in Newcastle-upon-Tyne A6127(M).

JUNCTION (1)

4m (6.5km) W on A66
Fox Hall Inn, East Layton. Dickensian coaching house; 11 rooms; excellent bar meals, good home cooking in restaurant (evenings and Sunday lunches only); very moderate charges. Tel: (0325) 718262.

JUNCTION (2)

DARLINGTON
2m (3km) NE on A66(M), then via Grange Road
Arts Centre In Vane Terrace; one of the liveliest and best-equipped arts/crafts studios and exhibition rooms in the region; restaurant.

3½m (5km) NE on A66(M) to Northgate Street

Railway Museum At

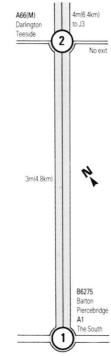

North Road station, originally the Stockton and Darlington passenger station of 1842; vintage engines on display, going back to Stephenson's *Locomotion;* souvenir shop, confectionery.

15m (24km) W on B6275 and A67
An easy road and worth the rather long detour for 3 major sights grouped in a small area: ornate, château-style

Bowes Museum, stern 14th-century **Barnard Castle** and even older **Bowes Castle.** They, and other feudal attractions of the County Palatine of Durham, are staging-posts on the **Bowes Trail** which traces the history of an influential family, the Queen Mother's ancestors.

A1(M) north: (3)-(6)

JUNCTION (3)

4m (6.5km) SE on A68
Darlington See Junction (2).

11m (16.5km) W on B6279 at Staindrop.

Seat of the Lords Barnard for 3 centuries, **Raby Castle** suggests lordly impregnability; fine timbered Baron's Hall, carriage collection in stables, yew hedges in garden and a kitchen worthy of Breughel's brush, all on the grand scale.

JUNCTION (4)

7m (11km) NW on A167 and W at Newton Aycliffe
Timothy Hackworth Museum, Shildon. Former home and workplace of Hackworth, another railway pioneer; museum has his 150-year-old locomotive *Sans Pareil;* from Shildon a footpath, the **Rail Trail,** on a disused Stephenson line.

JUNCTION (5)

6½m (10.5km) W on A689
Bishop Auckland Castle Medieval seat of the Durham prince-bishops; fine park and elaborate gatehouse; 1m (1.5km) N of town are Roman remains at **Binchester;** 1m (1.5km) W the

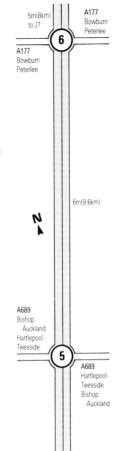

beautiful Saxon church of **Escomb.**

3m (5km) E on A689 near Sedgefield

Hardwick Hall Country Park A charming oasis in grim surroundings, always open; serpentine lake; children encouraged to sail boats and fish for tadpoles and minnows; lakeside paths; boardwalk trail; picnic and play areas.

JUNCTION (6)

DURHAM
3m (5km) NW on A177

Much to admire in medieval streets, under rockgirt **Castle** and

Cathedral above the Wear; riverside paths, old shops; **Fulling Mill** on Wear bank displays archaeology; **Oriental Museum** at Elvet Hill (left to A1050 entering city) is renowned for Chinese pottery, Japanese paintings, Persian arabesques and Egyptian sculptures. **Traveller's Rest restaurant,** 72 Claypath; good cuisine at reasonable prices; don't confuse with another place of same name nearby. Tel: (0385) 701 597.

A1(M) north: (7)-(9)

JUNCTION (7)

2½m (4km) W on A690
Slip-road gives easy
access to **Durham
Market Place** and
Traveller's Rest See
Junction (6)

*7m (11km) on A690 NE
and unclassified road NW,
crossing motorway; near
Pity Me*
Finchale Priory —
pronounced 'Finkle'; St
Godric's cell in pre-
Norman times, then a
retreat for monks of
Durham; extensive
ruins, pleasantly sited
above river Wear;
opposite, across
footbridge, **Cocken
Wood,** picnic area.

JUNCTION (8)

*5m (8km) W on A693,
signposted*

Beamish 'Acres of
nostalgia' says
advertisement, and no
exaggeration. Real-life
old times are assembled
in the park, round a
genuine 1920s street
brought in from old
Gateshead; farm
buildings, colliery
cottages, shops,
dentist's, law office etc.
accurately and

---

*1m(1.6km)
to J10*

*Washington-
Birtley*

Ⓢ A195
Washington
(S)

½m(0.8km)

⑨

A195
Washington-
Birtley

1m(1.6km)

A183
Sunderland
A167
Chester-le-
Street

⑧

A167
Chester-le-
Street

N
▲

6m(9.6km)

A690
Durham
Consett (A691)
Sunderland

⑦

*5m(8km)
to J6*

A690
Sunderland
Durham
Consett (A691)

---

convincingly
reconstructed; tramcars,
steam traction engines,

historic station and
period-piece train,
horse-drawn carriages;
Beamish is enthralling,
and still expanding, but
try to pick a quiet day —
this place is deservedly
popular.

*5m (8km) W on A6076
near Beamish*

Causey Arch Rocky
canyon, rushing waters,
wildflowers under the
'oldest railway bridge in
the world'; footpaths on
old waggonways,
explanatory notice-
boards; picnicking.

JUNCTION (9)

*3m (5km) E on A1231, the
south access road to
Washington New Town*

**Washington Waterfowl
Park** A Wildfowl Trust
centre, bordering river
Wear and furnished
with paths, bird feeding
stations and hides for
study of marshfowl;
reception building,
bookshop; insalubrious
neighbourhood.

A1(M) north: (10)-(13)

JUNCTION (10)

12m (19km) NW on A69

Hadrian's Wall This route takes you clear of Newcastle-upon-Tyne to **Rudchester** (Vindovala) and **Heddon-on-the-Wall,** where earthen rampart and ditch begin to be visible outside the city's urban sprawl; important Wall sights are still farther W.

JUNCTION (11)

WASHINGTON

1m (1.5km) E on A1231. Surrealist **shopping centre,** enterprising **arts centre** (Fatfield, District 7) with galleries and exhibitions proclaim the 'new town'; but there was once an 'old town' which gave Washington DC its name.

Washington Old Hall, ancestral home of George Washington's forebears, sleeps time away.

JUNCTION (12)
2m (3km) E on A195
Washington See Junction (11)

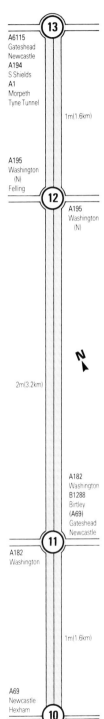

(13)

A6115
Gateshead
Newcastle
A194
S Shields
A1
Morpeth
Tyne Tunnel

1m(1.6km)

A195
Washington
(N)
Felling

(12)

A195
Washington
(N)

2m(3.2km)

A182
Washington
B1288
Birtley
(A69)
Gateshead
Newcastle

(11)

A182
Washington

1m(1.6km)

A69
Newcastle
Hexham

(10)

No exit

1m(1.6km)
to J9

JUNCTION (13)

NEWCASTLE-UPON-TYNE

4m (6.5km) W on A6115
Tourist Information Office in city centre; medieval city (when the Castle was really 'new') mixes with massive Victorian developments; ancient and modern in close juxtaposition at historic **Blackfriars,** now a centre for contemporary arts/crafts; **Guildhall,**

swing bridge on Tyne, **St Nicholas's Cathedral,** all central; **Laing Art Gallery,** near carpark on Princess Street, is outstanding for international, national and local works; **street markets,** Tue., Thur. and Sat., are a feature of Newcastle life; architecturally surprising **Eldon Square Centre,** all-pedestrian off Newgate Street, is the smart shopping centre.

Central motorway A6127(M), 2m (3km), Tyne Bridge to N exit roads, takes traffic clear of the city's heart.

5m (8km) N on A194

St Paul's Church, Jarrow. Simple building, revered throughout Christian world; home and workplace of Venerable Bede; recently celebrated 1300th anniversary.

A1(M)central:

Blythe to Hampole, 15m (24km)

This stretch of the Great North Road begins in Nottinghamshire and ends in South Yorkshire and is a bypass for the large and sprawling town of Doncaster. Mining villages which cluster along it are camouflaged in the great expanses of parkland and forest which once covered the whole region. Junctions are provisionally lettered, not numbered. At Junction B, on the edge of the Yorkshire coalfields, the A1(M) crosses the M18 motorway. It is a busy road day and night.

JUNCTION A

9m (14.5km) S on A1

National Mining Museum, Bothamsall. Permanent museum at a British Coal training centre; some unusually interesting relics of early mining days including resurrected ancient coal barge, old locomotives, pit pony harness and safety gear, old-fashioned timber headstocks, winding gear, primitive tools; also heavy machinery. Closed Mon.

6m (9.5km) E off A638 at Sutton-cum-Lound

Wetlands Waterfowl Reserve A newly-developed conservation area, already popular with duck, geese and swans from distant parts; binoculars for hire; butterflies and kingfishers in summer; plenty of wildlife in winter too (wrap up warmly and bring boots).

8m (13km) S on A1 and A614
The Dukeries Entrance to Clumber Park. See M1 Junction 30

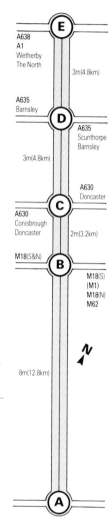

E
A638
A1
Wetherby
The North

3m(4.8km)

A635
Barnsley

D

A635
Scunthorpe
Barnsley

3m(4.8km)

A630
Doncaster

C

A630
Conisbrough
Doncaster

2m(3.2km)

M18(S&N)

B

M18(S)
(M1)
M18(N)
M62

N

8m(12.8km)

A

JUNCTION C

DONCASTER

2½m (4km) NE on A630
Extravagant pseudo-Gothic **St George's church,** off Churchway, like nothing you have seen before; **Cusworth Hall Museum,** Cusworth Lane, deals with Yorkshire industry, social life and canals in an appealing way (closed Fri.); also **history trail** through Cusworth Park.

4m (6.5km) SW on A630
Conisbrough Castle One of the knightly strongholds of old England with an imposing and stoutly-buttressed keep but little else; prominent in feudal quarrels of 12th century; featured in Scott's novel *Ivanhoe.*

JUNCTION D
3m (5km) E on A635
Doncaster
See Junction C

JUNCTION E

6m (10km) N on A1/A639
Nostell Priory See M62 Junction 32

4m (6.5km) N on A1
Barnsdale Bar Motorlodge Modern upmarket motel in wooded situation; 72 first-class rooms at first-class prices; take meals at adjacent mainroad service area, adequate choice and reasonably priced.

A1(M)south:

South Mimms to Colney Heath, 4m (7km) and Welwyn to Stotfold, 17m (27km)

This southernmost section of the 3 which raise the Great North Road to motorway status for short distances on its route between London and Newcastle-upon-Tyne is itself divided into 2 parts. It leaves London via Barnet and reverts to trunk road status as it passes through Hatfield. North of Hatfield it becomes the A1(M) again as far as a point on the Hertfordshire-Bedfordshire border just beyond Baldock.

The early parts of the route traverse the north London suburbs and touch at the 2 venerable 'garden cities' of the Home Counties, Welwyn (founded 1920) and Letchworth (1903). It also gives access to Stevenage, a 'new town' of the present era. Still regarded as the beginning of the main route to the north of England and Scotland, this part of the A1(M) trio is a busy highway at all times of day and night.

JUNCTION 1

2m (3km) NW via South Mimms on A6

Mosquito Aircraft Museum, London Colney. Aircraft, engines, components of various historic aircraft and auxiliary equipment; de Havilland aircraft of World War I and the Mosquito fighter-bomber of World War II are displayed (they were built here); claims to be oldest aircraft museum in Britain; some interesting aeronautical relics, but atmosphere is technical; shop; snacks. Open Thur., Sun. and bank holidays, summer only.

Map labels:
- 1m(1.6km) to J3
- A1001 Welham Green
- ② A1001 Welham Green
- 4m(6.4km)
- N
- M25 Harlow M11 Watford & M1 Potters Bar A1 London
- ①

JUNCTION 2

H **⊙**

5m (8km) W on A1 and A414
St Albans See M1 Junction 7

2m (3km) NW at A1/A414 intersection

Comet hotel Art-déco super-roadhouse of 1930s, now smart and sophisticated; some nostalgia around — it had links with the local aircraft industry; pleasant dining-room, big menu, rather pricey wines but otherwise reasonable. Tel: (020 72) 65411.

(Motorway ends and begins again at Junction 4)

A1(M) south: 4-6

JUNCTION 4

7m (11km) SW on A1 and A414
St Albans See M1
Junction 7

2m (3km) SE via Hatfield on A1000

Hatfield House Noble Jacobean mansion in a large park; celebrated as hotbed of politics (Cecils, Earls of Salisbury) since 1611; treasure-house of paintings, furniture, armour; chapel has antique stained glass; in garden, remains of 15th-century royal palace where Elizabeth I spent childhood; sundial garden, wilderness garden, knot garden; craft and horticultural exhibitions in summer; coffee shop. Closed in winter.

1½m (2.5km) E on A414

Old Mill House Museum, Mill Green, Hatfield. Local archaeological material; lively sequence of exhibitions of arts/crafts throughout summer; **Mill Green Watermill** (1762) next door is undergoing renovation.

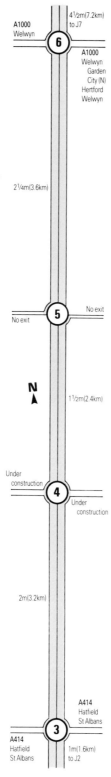

A1000
Welwyn

4½m(7.2km)
to J7

6

A1000
Welwyn
Garden
City (N)
Hertford
Welwyn

2¼m(3.6km)

5

No exit

No exit

N

1½m(2.4km)

Under
construction

4

Under
construction

2m(3.2km)

A414
Hatfield
St Albans

3

A414
Hatfield
St Albans

1m(1.6km)
to J2

JUNCTION 6

2½m (4km) W off B656
Shaw's Corner, Ayot St Lawrence. See M1 Junction 9

WELWYN GARDEN CITY
2m (3km) SE off A1000
Prettification of the urban plan, 1930s style; flower-beds, fountains, shrubs and careful landscaping employed to give fine vistas and cameos (but tour the centre slowly and in both directions to get the best of them); a place which has worn well, which students of town planning still come to see.

2m (3km) SW via Welwyn off A1000

Ayot St Peter Hilltop village amid foliage with **church** remarkable for decorative brickwork. From Ayot Green to Welwyn Garden City, across A1(M), stretches **Sherrards Park,** enclave of natural beauty with ancient oak avenues; footpaths, disused rail track; voluntary wardens patrol the woods.

JUNCTION 7

1½m (2.5km) W from A602, recrossing motorway, signposted

Knebworth House, Old Knebworth. Ornate pile of Jacobean character, loaded with mock-Gothic embellishments; overwhelming profusion of *objets d'art,* much of it high Victorian; Indian Durbar exhibition commemorates Viceroy Lytton; deer park; children's amusements; restaurant. Closed Mon. (except bank holidays) and in winter. The modern parts of **Knebworth village,** E of motorway, are a monument to architect Edwin Lutyens who built **Golf Club House, Homewood** and some cottages; he also laid out gardens of Knebworth House.

4m (6.5km) E off A602

Benington Lordship
Classic old garden and plant centre round evocative ruin of fortified dwelling; historical trail to amuse children while parents are buying plants. Open Sun. and Wed., May-July; Wed. only, Aug.-Oct.

A602
Hitchin
Stevenage
(N)

3m(4.8km)
to J9

(8)

A602
Hitchin
Stevenage
(N)

N

3m(4.8km)

A602
Stevenage
Knebworth
House

A602
Stevenage
Hertford
Knebworth
House

(7)

4½m(7.2km)
to J6

2m (3km) N on A602
Rook's Nest House, Weston Road, Stevenage. Strictly for E.M. Forster admirers; this was the novelist's childhood home and the house he called 'Howard's End'.

JUNCTION 8

5m (8km) E off B1037
Benington Lordship See Junction 7

GRAVELEY
1m (1.5km) NE on B197
Some attractive cottages in this tidy and well-maintained Hertfordshire village; small **medieval church;** fine 18th-century architecture of nearby **Grange** and **Gothic House;** chequered brick of **George and Dragon** worth studying.

HITCHIN
3m (5km) NW on A602
A town undeservedly neglected by tourists; though an important commercial and shopping centre with many up-to-date features, it retains a medieval nucleus with old **almshouses;** also half-timbered and Georgian brick **shops** and **houses;** unusually high buttresses and incomparable wood

carving at **St Mary's church,** town centre; several venerable inns, gabled and balustraded **Hitchin Priory,** a handsome Palladian town house with traces of monastic origins; well-kept public gardens, especially **Priory** and **Bancroft parks** along strangely-named River Hiz.

A1(M) south: *9-10*

JUNCTION 9

2m (3km) NW on A6141

First Garden City Museum, Norton Way South, Letchworth. Expounds the history of Garden City movement with plans of Letchworth, the prototype; housed in an interesting thatched house. N on Wilbury

Road, **Standalone Farm,** compact dairy, arable, poultry farm catering for visitors; sheep, pigs, milking demonstrations, wildfowl, blacksmith; natural history exhibitions. Closed in winter.

10

A1
The North
Peterborough
A507
Stotfold
Shefford

4m(6.4km)

N

A6141
Baldock
Letchworth

9

3m(4.8km)
to J8

A6141
Letchworth
Baldock

JUNCTION 10

ASHWELL
3m (5km) NE on byroads

Village of considerable antiquity and period charm; half-timbered Town House is the **Village Folk Museum,** one of the most comprehensive in S England (open Sun. only); **Merchant Taylors School,** 17th century; at ½m (1km) N, **springs** of Rhee or Cam, source of the river of Cambridge. **Three Tuns hotel,** Queen Anne house of character, delightfully variegated décor, hearty meals including traditional steak-and-kidney pie; moderate. Tel: (046 274) 2387.

7m (11km) NW off B658

Shuttleworth Collection, Old Warden. Old aircraft and vintage motor-cars assembled by young racing motorist R.O. Shuttleworth in 1930s, added·to by his mother and trustees after his death in World War II; venue for flying displays and veteran car rallies; the adjoining Shuttleworth family seat boasts a secluded riverside area called **Swiss Garden,** a delectable spot.

M2:

Strood to Faversham, 26m (41km)

This motorway pursues a wavering course through chalk cuttings on the northern slopes of the Downs, quite close to the Medway estuary, the Thames estuary, the Isle of Sheppey and the 'Isle' of Thanet, but not actually sighting the sea. The countryside is not quite 'garden of England' Kent, but it is fertile enough and pleasant in summer and there are numerous quiet villages and strips of orchards on the Downs. The 'Dover Road' has figured in history and romance, especially in Dickens. Canterbury, near the end of the motorway, with its cathedral's pinnacled tower visible a long way off, has been England's spiritual capital for more than 1000 years.

JUNCTION 1

6m (9.5km) NW on A2/A227

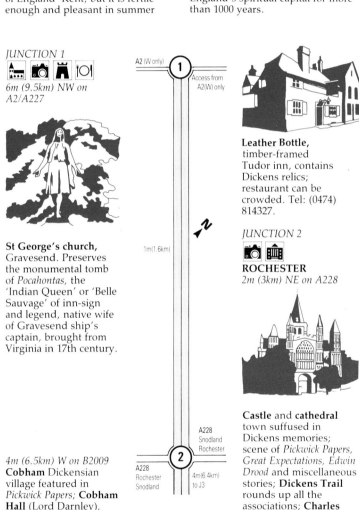

St George's church, Gravesend. Preserves the monumental tomb of *Pocahontas*, the 'Indian Queen' or 'Belle Sauvage' of inn-sign and legend, native wife of Gravesend ship's captain, brought from Virginia in 17th century.

4m (6.5km) W on B2009
Cobham Dickensian village featured in *Pickwick Papers*; **Cobham Hall** (Lord Darnley), Tudor mansion, now a girls' school, occasionally open to public; **Owletts** and **Tudor Yeoman's House,** Sole Street, (1m (1½km)) W, small but architecturally interesting Jacobean properties in care of National Trust;

A2 (W only)

① Access from A2(W) only

1m(1.6km)

A228 Snodland Rochester

② A228 Snodland Rochester

A228 Rochester Snodland

4m(6.4km) to J3

Leather Bottle, timber-framed Tudor inn, contains Dickens relics; restaurant can be crowded. Tel: (0474) 814327.

JUNCTION 2

ROCHESTER
2m (3km) NE on A228

Castle and **cathedral** town suffused in Dickens memories; scene of *Pickwick Papers, Great Expectations, Edwin Drood* and miscellaneous stories; **Dickens Trail** rounds up all the associations; **Charles Dickens Centre,** Eastgate House, cleverly evokes his life and work with tableaux and relics both charming and gruesome; **Guildhall Museum** offers escape from Dickens with its armoury and many quaint rural and domestic bygones.

M2: 3-5

JUNCTION 3

4m (6.5km) N on A229

Fort Amherst, Chatham. New and ambitious reconstruction of Georgian fortress spreads out behind Town Hall to **Chatham Lines,** the 18th-century defences put up to protect the dockyard from landward attack by French, who never came; gun batteries, redoubts, ammunition tunnels; resident 'garrison' enacts historical dramas at weekends in summer. Currently open Wed., Sat. and Sun., summer only, but days and times may be extended.

5m (8km) N on A229 and Dock Road

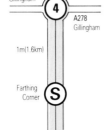

Chatham Dockyard Once a principal royal dockyard, no longer operational; museum facilities developing, meantime offers a walk through naval ship-repair history among unique Georgian and Victorian roperies, sail-lofts, rigging sheds; closed Mon., Tue. in summer, also Thur., Fri. in winter.

2m (3km) S on A229
Kit's Coty and **Bluebell Hill** See M20 Junction 6

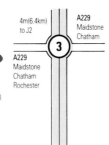

4m(6.4km)
to J2

A229
Maidstone
Chatham

3

A229
Maidstone
Chatham
Rochester

4m(6.4km)

A278
Gillingham

4

A278
Gillingham

1m(1.6km)

Farthing
Corner

S

3m(4.8km)

A249
Sittingbourne
Sheerness

5

A249
Maidstone
Sheppey
M20

10m(16km)
to J6

JUNCTION 5

6m (9.5km) SW off A249
Boxley See M20
Junction 7

4m (6.5km) NE off A249

Sittingbourne and Kemsley Light Railway, Mill Way, Sittingbourne. Narrow-gauge former paper-mill line from town to Swale channel, about 2m (3km); restored as steam-operated passenger railway; open Sun. and bank holidays throughout summer, also Wed. in Aug.

Dolphin Yard Sailing Barge Museum, Crown Quay Lane. Last resting-place of some old Thames sailing barges; souvenirs, bookshop; open Sun. and bank holidays in summer.

JUNCTION 6

FAVERSHAM

1m (1.5km) N on A251
Georgian town above
marshes and winding
creeks; **Fleur-de-Lys**
heritage centre, Preston
Street, recalls moments
of violent history,
including capture of
royal fugitive James II
and VII; Tudor
restorations in **Abbey
Street; gunpowder mills**
off Stonebridge Way,
oldest of their type in
existence (open most
Suns.); interesting
topography on marked
Saxon Shore footpath,
down creek from town
and along Swale inlet
(noted for marshfowl) to
Seasalter (7m (11km)).

JUNCTION 7

*1½m (2.5km) NE off A299
at Hernhill*
**Mount Ephraim
Gardens** Roses, topiary
work, Japanese rock
garden, craft centre,
orchard walks; newly-
planted vineyard; open
Sun. and bank holidays
only, May-early Sept.

*2½m (4km) NE off A299
at Dargate*

**Historic Motor and
Countryside Museum,**
Chapel Plantation.
Horseless carriages,
some weighty
specimens; carts and
waggons; rural
implements; teas; picnic
tables. Closed in winter.

A251
Ashford
Faversham

10m(16km)
to J5

6

A251
Ashford
Faversham

2m(3.2km)

►N

A2
Canterbury
Dover

A299
Margate
Ramsgate

7

*6m (9.5km) S off A2 on
byroads*

Chilham Castle Post-
Tudor castellated
mansion with an aspect
of chivalry, intensified
by medieval jousts (Sun.
and bank holidays in
summer); wreck of
original Norman castle
in grounds; birds of
prey; walks; restaurant.
Closed Nov.-Feb.

CANTERBURY

8m (13km) E on A2
Cathedral is Britain's
most distinguished
man-made structure,
with library with
Doomsday Book; city of

narrow streets within
stout walls and
archways; many
antiquated buildings,
including **West
Gateway, Christ Church
Gateway, St Martin's
church** and **Norman
keep**; Marlowe, Chaucer
and Sir Thomas More
associations; teashops
and antique shops
galore; 15th-century
**Falstaff inn; Old
Weavers' House** on
King's Bridge, St Peter's
Street, offers
handicrafts, good
patisseries and, from
garden steps, **river tours**
on city's little waterway
network. **George and
Dragon** inn (2m (3km)
downriver at Fordwich,
A28) serves admirable
buffet lunch, not
expensive.

M20: Swanley
to Bearsted, 24m (39km) and Ashford to Folkestone, 14m (22km)

The M20 is the principal motorway link between London and the Kent coast. It begins at a junction with the London ring motorway M25, 20m (32km) from central London. Skirting Maidstone and running beneath the ridge of the North Downs, it crosses the Weald of Kent and closely follows the route of the former trunk road A20 to Folkestone.

Between Bearsted and Ashford (Junction 8 and 9) the M20 is not yet open to traffic and no completion date for this 14m (22km) section has been given. Its terminus is at Folkestone, a major Channel port.

JUNCTION 1

2m (3km) NE via Swanley, across A225
St John's Jerusalem Garden, Sutton-at-Hone. Large moated garden beside Darent river, encircling former commandery of Knights Hospitallers; exquisite. Open Wed. in summer, closed in winter.

2½m (3.5km) S on A225
Eynsford Castle A solemn ruin, eternal reproach to Norman knight and descendants, all named William, all wild and dissolute; seventh William de Eynsford wrecked the place in a fit of drunken rage in 1312. Historic **Eynsford Bridge** crosses Darent river in nearby Eynsford village. Across A225 is

Lullingstone Roman Villa with museum, showplace of archaeology, example of gracious living 2nd and 3rd-century style.

JUNCTION 2

3m (5km) S off A227
Old Soar Manor, Plaxtol. Another style of gracious living, the Plantagenet, and

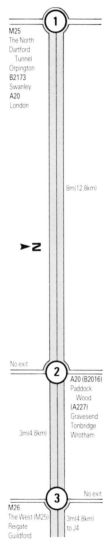

① M25
The North
Dartford
Tunnel
Orpington
B2173
Swanley
A20
London

8m(12.8km)

►2

② A20 (B2016)
No exit
Paddock
Wood
(A227)
Gravesend
Tonbridge
Wrotham

3m(4.8km)

③
No exit

M26
The West (M25)
Reigate
Guildford

3m(4.8km)
to J4

intensely uncomfortable it must have been; house (c. 1200) is small and bare; being stone-built, not wood-and-wattle, it has rarity value. **The Forge restaurant,** Plaxtol, 15th-century building; moderate prices for country cuisine. Tel: (0732) 810446.

2m (3km) S on A25
Ightham Village has several ancient **timber-framed houses** and 11th-century **church;** among tombs, 2 VCs, laid side by side.

4m (6.5km) S on A227

Ightham Mote, Ivy Hatch. Hollywood dream of historical romance setting, islanded in moat; chapel has painted ceiling; among best-known and most-visited of medieval manor-houses. Closed Tue., Thur., Sat. and all winter.

¼m (0.5km) N in Wrotham village, off A227
Access to **North Downs Way,** which here follows the **Pilgrims' Way** to Rochester and Canterbury. See M23 Junction 7

JUNCTION 4

3m (5km) NW via Snodland and byroads off A228

Coldrum Stones Bleak monoliths of a vanished Stone-Age race.

WEST MALLING

2m (3km) S on A228 Tudor, Jacobean, Georgian houses in village; also **Malling Abbey,** 16th-century on Saxon foundations, not visitable but visible and worth pausing for; **country park** S of village; **St Leonard's Tower** on wooded hillslope, ruin of early fortified manor-house; ½m (1km) S on Seven Mile Lane, Mereworth,

Parrot Breeding Centre, possibly unrivalled collection of parrots and parakeets. Closed in winter.

8m (13km) S on A228/B2015

Whitbread Hop Farm, Beltring. Big conglomeration of Victorian oast-houses; hops museum; agricultural, horses, crafts, machinery displays; hop gardens; pets' corner. Closed Mon. and all winter.

JUNCTION 5

2m (3km) N via A20, recrossing motorway **Aylesford Bridge** Photogenic old structure on Medway river; 1m

3m(4.8km) to J3

A228 New Hythe Rochester

4

A228 New Hythe Rochester Tonbridge

►Z

3m(4.8km)

A20 Aylesford

5

A20 Maidstone (W)

1m(1.6km)

A229 Maidstone Chatham Aylesford

6

A229 Maidstone Chatham Aylesford

2m(3.2km) to J7

(1.5km) N near A229, **Cobtree Manor Park;** country park with walks and picnic area.

1m (1.5km) SE off A20

Allington Castle 13th-century moated castle strategically placed in bend of Medway; fine gatehouse and inner courtyard; great hall and tithe barn; now a Carmelite retreat, immaculately kept; guided tours offered pm daily.

JUNCTION 6

2m (3km) S on A229 **Archbishop's Palace,** Maidstone. Elizabethan, with imposing banqueting hall; former official residence of Archbishops of Canterbury; in stables, Tyrwhitt-Drake Museum of Carriages, mostly horse-drawn, with step-by-step exposition of carriage construction.

1½m (2.5km) N on A229 **Cobtree Manor Park** See Junction 5

2½m (4km) N off A229

Kit's Coty Neolithic long barrow with 10-ton (10,000kg) roof stone on 3 uprights; **North Downs Way** crosses this site, with **Bluebell Hill** picnic area close by; views of Rochester, Chatham and Medway estuary.

35

M20: *7-10*

JUNCTION 7

2m (3km) SW on A249
Archbishop's Palace,
Maidstone. See
Junction 6

1m (1.5km) NE off A249
Boxley Sometime home
of Lord Tennyson;
stream which flows
from springs in vicarage
garden to ruined **Boxley
Abbey** is said to have
inspired his poem *The
Brook* — 'Men may come
and men may go/But I
go on for ever.'

JUNCTION 8

1m (1.5km) SW on A20

Leeds Castle In
situation, design and
scope, the most
breathtaking of Kent's
wonderful castles;
beloved home of 8
medieval queens;
French and English
décor, Impressionist
paintings reinforcing
resemblance to a Loire
château; lakes,
waterfalls, large heavily-
timbered park; Culpeper
(old-world, aromatic)
garden; vineyard with
buffet and wine-shop;
rare wildfowl; much
medieval heavy metal in
the rather incongruous
dog-collar collection at
gate house; like other
spectacular properties,
the place is not at its
best when seething with
crowds. Closed
weekdays in winter.

1m (1.5km) E on B2163
Hollingbourne Typical
Downland village with
access to **North Downs
Way;** inscription in
church requests prayers
for passengers in
passing aircraft.

36

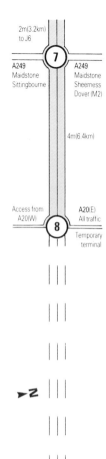

2m(3.2km)
to J6

7

A249
Maidstone
Sittingbourne

A249
Maidstone
Sheerness
Dover (M2)

4m(6.4km)

Access from
A20(W)

A20(E)
All traffic

8

Temporary
terminal

►Z

Projected

9

A20
All traffic

2m(3.2km)
to J10

**(Motorway ends and
begins again after
Junction 9)**

JUNCTION 10

2m (3km) NW on A292
Ashford Library,
Church Road, Ashford.
Railway research room
devoted to books,
magazines, pictures,
exhibitions on railway
topics.

7m (11km) W on B2077

Pluckley Saxon village
and feudal demesne
infested with ghosts of
various epochs; manor-
houses, farms, mill and
forge boast visitations
from, *inter alia,* Tudor
ladies, Cavaliers, a
Screaming Man, a
Hanged Colonel, a
Smiling Monk, a
Watercress Gypsy, a
Schoolmaster, a Miller
and a Coach and Pair.

TENTERDEN

12m (19km) SW on A28
Wide-verged, tree-lined,
gently-sloping **High
Street** is lined with
shops and houses from
c.1300 onwards; **St
Mildred's parish
church,** high 15th-
century tower with view
of English Channel;
Spots Farm Vineyard,
Small Hythe, guided
tours, shop, herb
garden, farm walk and
picnic area (closed Nov.-
Mar.); **Kent and East
Sussex Steam Railway,**
a 10m (16km) round
trip, most Sats. and/or
Suns. except Jan.-Mar.,
with shop, museum and
refreshments at Town
Station.

3m (5km) S on A2070

Kingsnorth Museum
Throwaway miscellany
hauled in by magpie
collector Joe Ripley; old
bottles, cigarette cards,
banknotes, farming and
wartime relics, penny-
farthing bike, World
War I motor-cycle
combination etc. — an
amazing and comic
pot-pourri.

*3m (5km) NE off A28 at
Wye*

Wife of Bath restaurant.
Established reputation;
painstaking cuisine,
careful service; set meals
moderately priced, *à la
carte,* expensive.
Tel: (0233) 812540.

*2m(3.2km)
to J9*

⊙ **10** ⊙

A292
Ashford

A292
Ashford
A20
Sellindge

7m(11.2km)

➤ Z

3m (5km) SE on A261

Hythe Station Start of
13½m (22km) Romney,
Hythe and Dymchurch
miniature railway, old-
established,
convincingly equipped,
said to be longest in
world; uncomfortable
for tall passengers;
steam and diesel power;
9 stations; models
exhibition, also
refreshments, at New
Romney station. Closed
weekdays in winter.

8m (13km) S on A259

Martello Tower,
Dymchurch. One of
several such defensive
towers on Kent and
Sussex coast, only this
one is open to
inspection.

11m (17.5km) S on A259

Greatstone station on
the Romney, Hythe and
Dymchurch Railway.
Seaside **stud farm** for
shire horses, Dunes
Road; wander at will;
foals usually on view;
donkey transport
available for children.
5m (8km) E of
Greatstone on Romney
Marsh,

astonishing
medieval **church** of St
Augustine at Brookland
(A2070) with detached
pagoda-like belfry;
decorated lead font,
very rare.

JUNCTION 11

2m (3km) S on B2068
Zoo park and terraced
gardens at Edwardian
country house of **Port
Lympne** (Sassoon
family); elephants,
tigers, rhino, tapirs,
snow leopards and
more; picnic site; on
cliff, with views across
Channel,

Lympne Castle,
medieval fortress
partly restored, with
museum of toys, dolls,
period costumes. Closed
in winter.

B2068
Lympne
(A20)
Canterbury

⊙ **11** ⊙

B2068
Canterbury
Hythe (A261)

*4m(6.4km)
to J12*

M20: *12-13*

JUNCTION 12

2m (3km) N on A260

4m(6.4km) to J11

A20 Cheriton Sandgate

A20 Cheriton Lyminge

Battle of Britain Museum, Hawkinge. New and expanding RAF and civil aircraft collection at once-famous fighter airfield, under skies which saw most of battle; pictures and a lot of twisted metal. Open Sun. and bank holidays, Sept.-June; Mon.-Sat. in July and Aug.

8m (13km) N on A260 and across A2 to Woolage (dual carriageway: necessitates U-turn at Barham X-roads 1m (1.5km) NW)

Treadwell Gallery, Denne Hill, Womenswold. Prestigious contemporary arts in stylistically chaotic mansion; sculpture garden; some startling and witty *jeux d'esprit*.

1m(1.6km)

JUNCTION 13

2m (3km) N on A260
Battle of Britain Museum See Junction 12

FOLKESTONE
1m (1.5km) S off A20
Large and versatile **arts centre** at Metropole, The Leas;

St Mary and St Eanswythe **parish church** has superb Harvey Window with plenty of crimson stained glass, Harvey being the locally-born physician who explained circulation of blood (1616);

Martello Tower; La Tavernetta restaurant, Leaside Court, superior Italian cuisine, seafood, moderately expensive. Tel: (0303) 54955.

A20 Dover Folkestone & Harbour

38

M23:

Caterham to Crawley, 16m (26km)

The M23 begins and ends on the Brighton road, swinging away from the A23 south of Croydon and rejoining it south of Crawley; and is furnished with a 2m (3km) spur to Gatwick airport. The route is scenically attractive. Its northern end is in Green Belt country on the North Downs and its southern sections wind across the lush Sussex countryside, where country-house gardens and garden centres jostle for elbow-room on every byroad.

The motorway is busy, as all roads are on the approaches to London, but is rarely congested. Junctions on the completed sections are numbered 7 to 11.

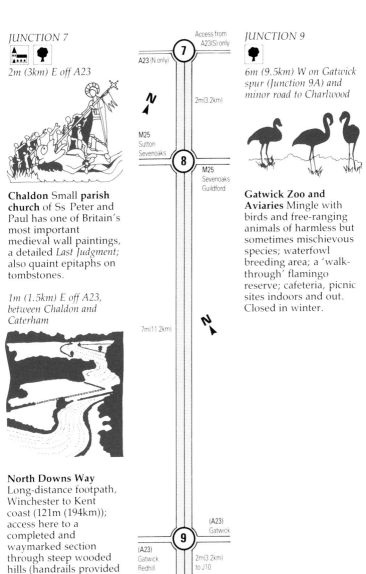

JUNCTION 7

2m (3km) E off A23

Chaldon Small **parish church** of Ss Peter and Paul has one of Britain's most important medieval wall paintings, a detailed *Last Judgment*; also quaint epitaphs on tombstones.

1m (1.5km) E off A23, between Chaldon and Caterham

North Downs Way Long-distance footpath, Winchester to Kent coast (121m (194km)); access here to a completed and waymarked section through steep wooded hills (handrails provided in places) with panoramic views.

JUNCTION 9

6m (9.5km) W on Gatwick spur (Junction 9A) and minor road to Charlwood

Gatwick Zoo and Aviaries Mingle with birds and free-ranging animals of harmless but sometimes mischievous species; waterfowl breeding area; a 'walk-through' flamingo reserve; cafeteria, picnic sites indoors and out. Closed in winter.

Access from A23(S) only

A23 (N only)

2m(3.2km)

M25 Sutton Sevenoaks

M25 Sevenoaks Guildford

7m(11.2km)

(A23) Gatwick

(A23) Gatwick Redhill

2m(3.2km) to J10

A264
Crawley
East Grinstead

2m(3.2km)
to J9

JUNCTION 10

4m (6.5km) E on B2028 at Newchapel

A264
Crawley
Horsham
East Grinstead

JUNCTION 11

4m (6.5km) S on A23

London Temple
Headquarters of British and European Latter-day Saints (Mormons); stark art-deco temple block with large pseudo-Elizabethan manor house close by.

6m (9.5km) E on A264
Sackville College, East

Grinstead.
Architecturally pleasing group of Jacobean almshouses in sandstone; reminiscent of a Belgian *béguinage;* open to visitors.
Gravetye Manor hotel, Sharpthorne, East Grinstead; Tudor house in a well-known 'wild' garden; *Relais de Campagne* approved restaurant, *haute cuisine* and wines to match. Tel: (0342) 810567.

5m (8km) SE on A264 and B2028, signposted
Wakehurst Place, Ardingly. Glorious jewel in National Trust crown; renowned for gardens, built up by Gerald Loder 1903-1936, with plants and shrubs from southern hemisphere; rock walk among writhing tree-roots and creeping plants; gorgeous springtime and late springtime displays of blooms in deep ravines and woods.

Nymans Garden,
Handcross. Another horticultural wonder of the Sussex Weald, a composition of intimate and romantic nooks and corners; walled garden, sunken garden; huge screens of azaleas, rhododendrons, magnolias, hydrangeas; topiary work and majestic cedars; ruins of house, fountains and follies complete the picture; teahouse. Closed in winter.

5m (8km) SE off A23 via Ardingly (B2028)

Bluebell Railway,
Horsted Keynes. The little train everyone has heard of; steam line to **Sheffield Park,** 5m (8km), through luxuriant foliage of a very civilized countryside; carriage sheds at Horsted Keynes terminus, loco sheds at Sheffield Park terminus; latter station is ½m (1km) from National Trust's well-known woodlands and formal gardens of Sheffield Park. Closed in winter.

5m(8km)

A23
Pease Pottage
Brighton

M25:
London outer ring, 116m (186km)

The M25 provides a non-stop route round London from Dartford in Kent to Grays in Essex. (Those towns are linked across the Thames by the Dartford tunnel and approaches (4m (7km)) with toll.) Although the motorway is nowhere more than 20m (32km) from Westminster Bridge in London, it passes through some agreeable countryside in Kent and Surrey between Junctions 3 and 10 and again through pleasantly rural districts of Essex between Junctions 26 and 28. These sections are not as a rule heavily trafficked. Elsewhere, however, London's orbital motorway has been under

criticism from the time its first sections were opened. It has acquired a reputation for increasing congestion in the suburbs. Queues around Junctions 1 and 31, where traffic merges for the Dartford tunnel and pauses for the toll, sometimes stretch back for several miles.

It is not a route for the weary or the absent minded; the traffic flow often resembles a cavalry charge, and concentration is needed. The Junctions are numbered clockwise from Dartford. At Junction 19 there is a 1m (1½km) spur to Hunton Bridge roundabout, Watford.

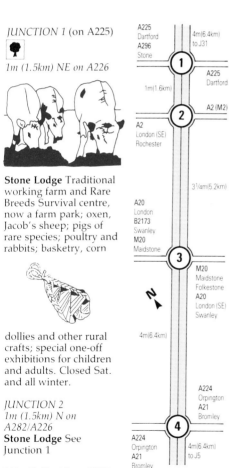

JUNCTION 1 (on A225)

1m (1.5km) NE on A226

Stone Lodge Traditional working farm and Rare Breeds Survival centre, now a farm park; oxen, Jacob's sheep; pigs of rare species; poultry and rabbits; basketry, corn

dollies and other rural crafts; special one-off exhibitions for children and adults. Closed Sat. and all winter.

JUNCTION 2
1m (1.5km) N on A282/A226
Stone Lodge See Junction 1

1½m (2.5km) S on A225
St John's Jerusalem Garden See M20 Junction 1

A225 Dartford A296 Stone

4m(6.4km) to J31

1

A225 Dartford

1m(1.6km)

2

A2 (M2)

A2 London (SE) Rochester

3¼m(5.2km)

A20 London B2173 Swanley M20 Maidstone

3

M20 Maidstone Folkestone A20 London (SE) Swanley

N

4m(6.4km)

A224 Orpington A21 Bromley

4

A224 Orpington A21 Bromley

4m(6.4km) to J5

JUNCTION 3
Junction with M20 Junction 1; access to Swanley

2m (3km) NE via Swanley, across A225
St John's Jerusalem Garden See M20 Junction 1

2½m (4km) S on A225
Eynsford Castle, Eynsford Bridge, Lullingstone Roman Villa. See M20 Junction 1

JUNCTION 4
1½m (2.5km) E on A225
Lullingstone Roman Villa, Eynsford Bridge, Eynsford Castle. See M20 Junction 1

M25: *5-8*

JUNCTION 5

Junction with M26
Junction 4, but access
also to A21.

*11m (17.5km) S on A21
and B2188*

Penshurst Place Huge
feudal manor (Viscount
de l'Isle) with vast Great
Hall; a spacious opulent
house, very much lived
in; Tudor gardens and
terraces; hedged
enclosures a special
feature; self-service
restaurant. Closed Mon.
(except bank holidays)
and in winter.

*7m (11km) S on A21 and
B2042*

Bough Beech Important
conservation area round
large reservoir, creation
of which has brought
countless migratory
birds; nature trail;
woodland; information
centre in picturesque
abandoned oast-house.
Open Wed., Sat., Sun.,
summer only.

4m (6.5km) W off A25

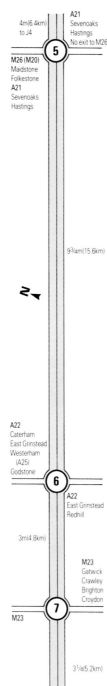

4m(6.4km)
to J4

A21
Sevenoaks
Hastings
No exit to M26

⑤

M26 (M20)
Maidstone
Folkestone
A21
Sevenoaks
Hastings

9¾m(15.6km)

A22
Caterham
East Grinstead
Westerham
(A25)
Godstone

⑥

A22
East Grinstead
Redhill

3m(4.8km)

M23
Gatwick
Crawley
Brighton
Croydon

⑦

M23

3¼m(5.2km)

A217
Sutton
Reigate
Redhill (A25)

⑧

A217

7m(11.2km)
to J9

Squerryes Court
Perfectly-proportioned
17th-century country
house in mellow red
brick; has links with
General Wolfe, hero of
Quebec; neat garden.
Close by, off B2026,
three National Trust
properties; **Chartwell**
(Sir Winston Churchill

relics and the garden
wall he built); **Quebec
House** (General Wolfe);
and the delightful
Emmetts Gardens
(closed in winter).

JUNCTION 6
7m (11km) E on A25
Squerryes Court See
Junction 5

¼m (0.5km) N on A22
Access to **North Downs
Way** See M23 Junction 7

JUNCTION 8

REIGATE
2m (3km) S on A217
Ancient town now
overshadowed by more
populous Redhill;
Reigate Priory,
medieval monastic
settlement and
afterwards site of Tudor
mansion of Lord
Howard of Effingham
(his reward for defeating
the Scots at Flodden),
with fine decorated
staircase and elaborate
iron gates, is now local
museum; ancient
windmill on Reigate
Heath serves as
Nonconformist chapel;
Gatton Manor is now a
school but public paths
cross breezy expanses of
park; **Baron's Cave,**
under Castle Hill, has
18th-century graffiti.

JUNCTION 9

2m (3km) N on A243

Chessington Zoo
Incorporates funfair and circus (summer only); safari skyway gives birds'-eye views; good family entertainment.

4m (6.5km) S on A24
Box Hill Wooded ridge above pastures, high point of North Downs with views of South Downs 24m (38km) away to S; centre for excellent walks between Nower Wood to NE and Abinger to SW; **North Downs Way** crosses hill; serene and fragrant spot on a quiet day.

2m (3km) W on A245
St Mary the Virgin parish church, Stoke d'Abernon. Stands apart on river bank; archaic stones built into it, Roman they say; a goulash of ecclesiastical décor, including Jacobean pulpit, traces of wall painting, 15th-century bell by famous female bell-founder Joanna Sturdy and brasses of d'Abernon tombs, one of which, intricately engraved, is the oldest in England (1277).

JUNCTION 10

3m (5km) E on A245
St Mary the Virgin parish church See Junction 9

2m (3km) W off A3
Wisley Garden Riot of colour from

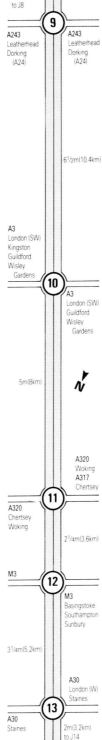

- 7m(11.2km) to J8
- ⑨
- A243 Leatherhead Dorking (A24) | A243 Leatherhead Dorking (A24)
- 6½m(10.4km)
- A3 London (SW) Kingston Guildford Wisley Gardens
- ⑩
- A3 London (SW) Guildford Wisley Gardens
- 5m(8km)
- A320 Woking A317 Chertsey
- ⑪
- A320 Chertsey Woking
- 2¼m(3.6km)
- M3 | ⑫ | M3 Basingstoke Southampton Sunbury
- 3¼m(5.2km)
- A30 London (W) Staines
- ⑬
- A30 Staines | 2m(3.2km) to J14

rhododendrons, azaleas, ornamental trees, herbaceous and rock plants; fruit gardens and glasshouses; practical horticultural demonstrations; garden centre; shop; cafeteria open in summer.

JUNCTION 11

3m (5km) E off A320
Brooklands Historic motor-racing circuit, deserted now except for ghost of Percy Lambert (killed in a race, 1913), whose roaring engine and squealing tyres echo round the track — according to some. 1m (1.5km) E on B365, **Whiteley Village,** built by the 'Universal Provider' (drapery mogul William Whiteley) in Edwardian days as retirement homes for the superannuated — a strange little complex of buildings by all the best architects of the day, with plenty of greenery.

1½m (2.5km) N on A320
Sunbury, Thorpe Park, Shepperton See M3 Junction 1

JUNCTION 13
1½m (2.5km) W on A308
Runnymede See M4 Junction 5

6m (9.5km) NW off A308
Windsor See M4 Junction 6

3m (5km) SW off A30
Savill and Valley Gardens See M4 Junction 5

8m (13km) W on B3022
Windsor Safari Park See M4 Junction 6

M25: 14-18

JUNCTION 14
3m (5km) E on A3113
Petit Four restaurant,
Terminal 4, Heathrow.
See M4 Junction 4

JUNCTION 17

4m (6.5km) W to A413
Milton's Cottage See
M40 Junction 2

*2m (3km) W unclassified,
signposted, at Newland
Park*

**Chiltern Open Air
Museum** 500 years of
rustic architecture
assembled in buildings
of various kinds from
barns to cottages; nature
trail; picnic area;
cafeteria. Open Wed.,
Sun. and bank holidays,
summer only.

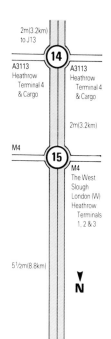

2m(3.2km)
to J13

14

A3113
Heathrow
Terminal 4
& Cargo

A3113
Heathrow
Terminal 4
& Cargo

2m(3.2km)

M4

15

M4
The West
Slough
London (W)
Heathrow
Terminals
1, 2 & 3

5½m(8.8km)

N

M40
Oxford
Uxbridge
London (W)

16

M40
Uxbridge
London (W)
Oxford

5¾m(9.2km)

(A412)
Maple Cross

17

A412
Maple Cross
Rickmansworth

1½m(2.4km)

A404

18

A404
Amersham
Chorleywood
Rickmansworth

3m(4.8km)
to J19

JUNCTION 18

CHENIES
2m (3km) NW on A404
Parklike **green** of good-
looking village slopes to
church; manor-house
(Dukes of Bedford in
Elizabethan times) is

44

restored and furnished
to the standard of its
Tudor heyday, when
royalty frolicked here;
topiary work; physic
garden; underground
passages; turf maze (ie
pattern on the ground)
of modern construction.

Bedford Arms, Chenies;
restaurant offers
extensive menu,
generous helpings;
expensive.
Tel: (092 78) 4335.

2m (3km) SE on A404

Moor Park Grandiose
Palladian hall with
gatehouses and
outbuildings in
proportion; old pleasure
grounds; Italian-style
gardens, where first
'apricocks' were grown
(c. 1760); after passing
through hands of feudal
and merchant barons,
the last being Lord
Leverhulme, Moor Park
became a golf club; hall
is now clubhouse and
great park of feudal
memories is known
chiefly as venue for *Bob
Hope Golf Classic.* Closed
Sat. pm, Sun. and
during golf
championships.

JUNCTION 19

1½m (2.5km) S via M25 spur and A411
Cheslyn Gardens See M1 Junction 5

2m (3km) S via M25 spur and A411

Cassiobury Park,
Watford. Attractive family-type leisure area with many walks and picnic sites; on W side, Whippendell Woods, with trails among handsome broad-leaved trees; Gade river and Union Canal wind through park, narrow boat from Ironbridge Lock cruises a pleasant and not at all monotonous stretch of river and canal, a 75-min. trip (Sun. throughout summer, also Tue. and Thur. in Aug.).

JUNCTION 23
2m (3km) NW off A6
Mosquito Aircraft Museum See A1(M) (south) Junction 1

JUNCTION 24

7m (11km) N on A1000
Hatfield House See A1(M) (south) Junction 4

3m (5km) SE on A1005

The Butterfly Centre,
Theobalds Park Road, Enfield. Tropical

glasshouses with moths and butterflies, promoting work of British Butterfly Conservation Society; plants sold and advice given on starting a butterfly garden.

JUNCTION 25

6m (9.5km) N on A10 and A1170

Dobbs Weir N end of **Lee Valley Leisure Park,** 23m (36km) strip of public parkland accompanying Lee river (sometimes spelled Lea) from Ware in Hertfordshire to Hackney Marsh in London's East End. Dobbs Weir, expanse of landscaped river meadows, is junction of country walks which stretch intermittently through whole park along rivers, reservoirs and river-locks; 1m (1.5km) N of Weir, **Rye House** (see M11 Junction 7); S of Weir, B194 skirts open, hilly **Clayton Hill Country Park** and pools, footpaths, picnic sites of **Fishers Green** en route to **Hayes Hill Farm** (see Junction 26) and **Waltham Abbey** (see Junction 26). The Lee Valley Park has its lidos, marinas and caravan parks but the section N of motorway is not overburdened with litter or glitter; the section S of motorway, especially **Picketts Lock Centre,** Edmonton (3m (5km) S on A1010 and B137 from Junction 25), has more entertainment and sporting facilities but less peace and quiet.

45

JUNCTION 26

1½m (2.5km) NW on A121

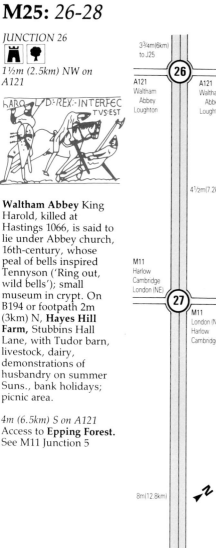

Waltham Abbey King Harold, killed at Hastings 1066, is said to lie under Abbey church, 16th-century, whose peal of bells inspired Tennyson ('Ring out, wild bells'); small museum in crypt. On B194 or footpath 2m (3km) N, **Hayes Hill Farm**, Stubbins Hall Lane, with Tudor barn, livestock, dairy, demonstrations of husbandry on summer Suns., bank holidays; picnic area.

4m (6.5km) S on A121
Access to **Epping Forest.** See M11 Junction 5

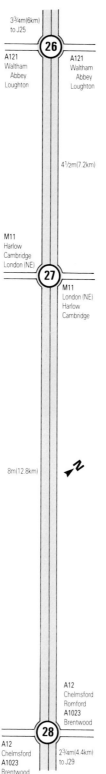

26

A121
Waltham
Abbey
Loughton

A121
Waltham
Abbey
Loughton

3¾m(6km)
to J25

4½m(7.2km)

M11
Harlow
Cambridge
London (NE)

27

M11
London (NE)
Harlow
Cambridge

8m(12.8km)

A12
Chelmsford
Romford
A1023
Brentwood

28

A12
Chelmsford
A1023
Brentwood

2¾m(4.4km)
to J29

JUNCTION 28

2½m (4km) N off A12
Weald Country Park
Small area of woodland; game; ponds, walking, riding.

3m (5km) E on A128 via Brentwood
Thorndon Country Park
Large area, mostly woodland, with pleasant walks; fishing; on S side, good views of Thames estuary; on E side, a dry ski-slope.

2m (3km) S on B186
St Mary Virgin church, Great Warley. Admired by most, condemned by a few, for its striking art-nouveau architecture and decoration.

10m (16km) N on A128
St Andrew's log church, Greensted. See M11 Junction 7

8m (13km) NE on A12

Furze Hill restaurant, Margaretting. Charming house and garden redeem it from roadhouse character; heated pool for customers; ambitious menus; disco dinner Fri., dinner-dance Sat., music with lunch Sun.; invigorating atmosphere and not expensive, considering amenities offered. Tel: (0277) 354755.

JUNCTION 29

BASILDON
*8m (13km) E on
A127/A128*
Not an obvious tourist
venue, but Rowland
Emmett (whimsical little
trains etc.) precinct
Pussywillow III attracts
visitors; at 1m (1.5km)
SW, **Langdon Hills,**
high pastures
commanding views of
Thames estuary, include
Westley Heights and

**One Tree Hill country
parks;** grassland,
woodland, thorn scrub,
sandy heath; ranger
service; guided walks;
information centre.

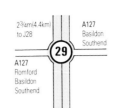

2¾m(4.4km) to J28

A127 Basildon Southend

29

A127 Romford Basildon Southend

N ▲

5½m(8.8km)

A13 Tilbury

30

A13 Dagenham Tilbury A282 (A126) Grays (A1306)

¾m(1.2km)

No access (use J30)

No exit

31

A13 Dagenham London A282

JUNCTION 30

2m (3km) W on A13

Rainham Hall Four-
square early Georgian
mansion; period
panelling; notable
wrought-iron gates;
National Trust.

10m (16km) NE on A13
Langdon Hills See
Junction 29

*8m (13km) SE on
A13/A126*

Tilbury Fort Remains of
fortifications and double
moat of important
Thames stronghold at
period of Dutch wars,
mid-17th century; good
viewpoint for endlessly
absorbing life of the
river.

*JUNCTION 31
6m (10km) SE via Grays
on A282 and A126*
Tilbury Fort See
Junction 30

*5m (8km) S on A282 and
A226 via Dartford tunnel
(toll)*
Stone Lodge See
Junction 1

M26:

Wrotham to Riverhead, 10m (16km)

Crossing the most typical countryside of the 'garden of England', the M26 completes a motorway triangle of which the M20 and M25 (meeting at Swanley) are the other two sides. Its terminal junctions are not numbered. Its one intermediate junction is numbered 2A to distinguish it from the adjacent Junction 2 on the M20. This is not a route for London-bound motorists, only for those travelling between Surrey and Kent. It is therefore free as a rule of the congestion which is common at certain times of the day on neighbouring motorways.

JUNCTION 2A

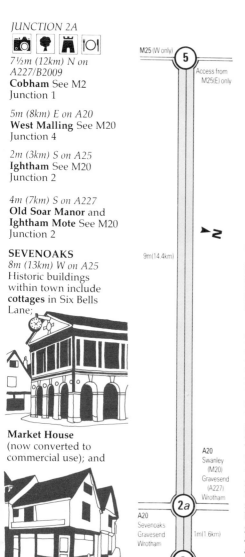

7½m (12km) N on A227/B2009
Cobham See M2 Junction 1

5m (8km) E on A20
West Malling See M20 Junction 4

2m (3km) S on A25
Ightham See M20 Junction 2

4m (7km) S on A227
Old Soar Manor and **Ightham Mote** See M20 Junction 2

SEVENOAKS
8m (13km) W on A25
Historic buildings within town include **cottages** in Six Bells Lane;

Market House
(now converted to commercial use); and

Red House, known to Jane Austen, in Upper High Street.

The Vine
has been a cricket ground since 1740s; exquisite gardens attached. Picnic area and Weald viewpoint in charming surroundings on **One Tree Hill,** 1½m (2½km) S. Of several National Trust properties in neighbourhood, chief is

Knole (Sackville-Wests) off Upper High Street; largest country house in Kent, with park to match; renowned furnishings, especially 17th-century English furniture; associated with the Bloomsbury group and other literary coteries. Closed Mon., Tue. except bank holidays; closed in winter. **Royal Oak restaurant,** Upper High Street; intimate surroundings, carefully-balanced set menu; good home-made *patés* and *quiches* in wine bar; all charges moderate. Tel: (0732) 451109.

1m (1.5km) N on A20
North Downs Way See M20 Junction 2

M25 (W only) — 5
Access from M25(E) only

9m(14.4km)

N

A20 Swanley (M20) Gravesend (A227) Wrotham

A20 Sevenoaks Gravesend Wrotham — 2a

1m(1.6km)

3
M20 (E only)

M27:

Cadnam to Cosham, 27m (43km)

The M27 begins in the New Forest near the Rufus Stone. It crosses the head of Southampton Water, the northern suburbs of Southampton and the Hamble river and runs along the northern side of Portsmouth harbour. Thus it has views of Britain's major mercantile harbour and Britain's principal naval port. On the motorway map it looks like the base-line on which the whole system is erected; but it will be years before new construction bridges the gaps which separate it from the M5, M3 and M25. At present there are 2 south-going spurs into Southampton and Portsmouth respectively — see M271 and M275. Another short motorway near its eastern terminus takes traffic clear of the Portsmouth conurbation — see A3(M).

JUNCTION 1

MINSTEAD

1½m (2.5km) S off A31
Forest village and centre of crafts; **Furzey Gardens,** masses of shrubbery, azaleas and rhododendrons predominating; popular **Honeypot tearoom** (coffee and lunches too); **Selwood Gallery,** timber and thatch, displays local woodcrafts, pottery, metalwork, paintings; **Honeysuckle Cottage,** snug dwelling built from timbers of Tudor ship. At ½m (1km) across A31, **Rufus Stone,** Stoney Cross, marks spot where William II was shot, maybe deliberately, by an arrow while hunting (1100 AD).

BREAMORE

8m (13km) W on B3078 and A338
Pleasant village clothed in woodland, with **Saxon church;**

Breamore House, stately Tudor mansion, is beautifully furnished and has a worthwhile carriage collection in stables; **Countryside Museum** gives lavish coverage of

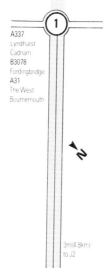

A337
Lyndhurst
Cadnam
B3078
Fordingbridge
A31
The West
Bournemouth

3m(4.8km)
to J2

life and leisure in olden times (closed Mon., Fri., and all winter).

ROCKBOURNE

14m (22.5km) W on B3078

Perhaps the prettiest of S Hampshire villages in chalk valley where in 1944 **Rockbourne Roman Villa,** largest in Britain, was discovered; well-preserved mosaic flooring; **museum** of finds, including jewelry. Closed in winter.

3m (5km) S on A337
Forest Lodge, Pikes Hill. Charming country **hotel** and **restaurant** on edge of Lyndhurst; 20 rooms; swimming pool; overlooks golf course; from bar snacks to candlelit dinner, food and wines are of uniformly high standard and not too pricey. Tel: (042 128) 3677.

M27: 2-4

JUNCTION 2

🌳 🏰 🏛️

2m (3km) NW on A36

Paultons Park
Amusement park with all the latest (and noisiest) in entertainments; thrills, spills and fun of fair, or walks beside river and lake, through woods and

'gypsy encampment' and among exotic animals and birds; gardens neatly laid out. At 1m (1.5km) N off A36, just out of earshot, is East Wellow country churchyard and **grave of**

Florence Nightingale.

4m (6.5km) N on A31

Broadlands, Romsey. Like a mini-Buckingham Palace; fine house with gardens sloping to River Test is almost overshadowed by

memorial exhibition to distinguished late occupants, Admiral of the Fleet Earl Mountbatten and Edwina, Countess Mountbatten. More extravagance, of the ecclesiastical kind, in **Romsey Abbey** nearby, a Norman foundation.

JUNCTION 4
10m (16km) N on A33
Winchester See M3
Junction 10

A36
Salisbury
Bristol

3m (4.8km)
to J1

2

A31
Romsey
A36
Salisbury

2m(3.2km)

M271
Southampton
Docks &
Ferries

3

M271
Southampton
Docks &
Ferries
A3057
Romsey

2m(3.2km)

N

S Rownhams

1½m(2.4km)

No exit **4**

A33
London
Midlands
Winchester

1m(1.6km)

4 No exit

A33
London
Midlands
Winchester

1m(1.6km)
to J5

JUNCTION 5

3m (5km) N on A335 and B3037
Bishopstoke Delightful river walks along loops of Itchen river and canal, with preserved locks; rich spread of plants; some wildlife.

A335
Eastleigh
Airport

1m(1.6km)
to J4

⑤

A335
Eastleigh
Airport

Botleigh Grange hotel, impressive 16th-century country house, traditional English dishes, also set-price help-yourself carvery and short but select wine-list; extremely good value in moderate to expensive range. Tel: (048 92) 5611.

JUNCTION 8

4m (6.5km) W on A3025
Southampton docks and waterfront. See M271

½m (1km) N, signposted
Upper Hamble Country Park See Junction 7

2m (3km) S off A3025

Netley Extensive remains of 13th-century Cistercian **abbey,** off Grange Road;

Royal Victoria Country Park in grounds of Britain's first military hospital, tree-lined grounds with excellent view across Southampton Water, picnic places on seafront, chapel and Heritage Exhibition (Florence Nightingale associations); **Lower Swanwick,** nearby on Hamble river, was setting for TV serial *Howard's Way.*

JUNCTION 7

BOTLEY
2m (3km) E on A334
Tourist village of shops and restaurants on Hamble river; 12th-century **church; memorial** to William Cobbett *(Rural Rides);* **Upper Hamble Country Park,** restful environment and good walking along broad winding stream; in park

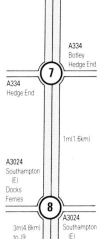

Hampshire Farm Museum exhibits old-time agricultural activities (buildings more interesting than their contents) and Queen Elizabeth II Activities Centre concentrates on facilities for handicapped and disabled. **Purbani tandoori restaurant,** The Square, Botley; fantastic range of Indian specialties with courteous service; prices most reasonable. Tel: (048 92) 3161. At 1m (1.5km) E at Hedge End,

4m(6.4km)

A334
Botley
Hedge End

⑦

A334
Hedge End

1m(1.6km)

A3024
Southampton
(E)
Docks
Ferries

⑧

A3024
Southampton
(E)

3m(4.8km)
to J9

M27: *9-11*

JUNCTION 9

6m (9.5km) S off A27

Solent Butterfly House,
Stubbington. Small sub-
tropical garden with
butterflies; insect house;
sculpture gallery
specializing in wildlife
wood carvings. Closed
in winter.

JUNCTION 10

9m (14.5km) N on A333

Bishop's Waltham
Ruins of palace which in
earlier times was
residence of Winchester
bishops; undergoing
long-term restoration.

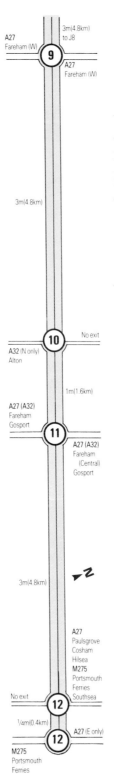

A27
Fareham (W)

9

A27
Fareham (W)

3m(4.8km)
to J8

3m(4.8km)

10 No exit

A32 (N only)
Alton

1m(1.6km)

A27 (A32)
Fareham
Gosport

11

A27 (A32)
Fareham
(Central)
Gosport

3m(4.8km)

A27
Paulsgrove
Cosham
Hilsea
M275
Portsmouth
Ferries
Southsea

No exit **12**

¼m(0.4km)

12 A27 (E only)

M275
Portsmouth
Ferries

DROXFORD
7m (11km) N on A32
Village of Meon valley
whose **railway station,** a
D-day (1944) invasion
HQ, is preserved as a
monument. 2m (3km) W
of village on byroad to

Dean, **Hampshire
Bowman inn** maintains
old archery traditions
with summer shoot-outs
(usually Sun.); 2m
(3km) E on road to East
Meon, **Old Winchester
Hill** has nature trails
and superb views over
Solent and Isle of
Wight.

JUNCTION 11

7m (11km) S on A32

Submarine Museum,
Gosport. Development
of underwater craft and
warfare at Royal Navy's
submarine school;
models, pictures,
trophies; H.M.S.
Alliance, a real World
War II submarine, high
and dry but in
operational state and
open to full inspection.
Closed Christmas Eve,
Christmas Day.

M271:
Upton to Southampton West, 2½m (3.5km)

The M271 crosses the M27 for Southampton and ends on the western side of the city at the head of Southampton Water. The district through which it passes is almost entirely built over; Totton, near the terminus, is heavily industrialized.

JUNCTION 3

📷 🏛 🎭

SOUTHAMPTON
3m (5km) E on A35
Large and busy maritime city, pleasingly laid out for the most part, with impressive modern **Civic Centre; Art Gallery** in civic centre is generally regarded as best outside London for old masters, impressionists and contemporaries; **Maritime Museum,** Wool House, Bugle Street, recalls city's historic links with transatlantic trade, notably Cunarders and *Titanic*; **Tudor House,** also Bugle Street, authentic merchant's property appropriately furnished and having 16th-century garden;

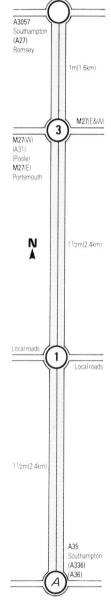

Hall of Aviation, Saltmarsh Road near Continental ferry port, commemorates the Solent's historic links with seaplanes, flying-boats and Spitfire production, beautifully-arranged exhibition of some unusual aircraft (closed Mon.); **harbour cruises** from Town Quay go down Southampton Water, always an enthralling scene for those with salt in veins.

A3057
Southampton
(A27)
Romsey

1m(1.6km)

M27(E&W)

3

M27(W)
(A31)
(Poole)
M27(E)
Portsmouth

N
▲

1½m(2.4km)

Local roads

1

Local roads

1½m(2.4km)

A35
Southampton
(A336)
(A36)

A

JUNCTION 1
(Junction with A3057 near Upton)
3½m (5.5km) N on A3057
Broadlands and **Romsey Abbey.** See M27 Junction 2

JUNCTION A

📷 🌳

(Terminus on A36)
3m (5km) E on A3024
Southampton See Junction 1

1m (1.5km) W on A336

Eling Tide Mill, Totton (beside Toll Bridge). Only 3 such mills survive, this the only one that works; tide-operated flour mill; tortuous guided tour, possibly some waiting (if so, **Goatee picnic park** and foreshore are close at hand). Closed in winter.

4m (6.5km) SW on A35
New Forest Butterfly Farm, Longdown near Ashurst. One of the first established in Britain; tropical garden supports exotica, country garden has native species; dragonfly ponds; waggon-rides May-Sept., according to demand; unlike most butterfly farms, this one is secluded from the world in acres of greenwood. Closed in winter.

M275:

Cosham to Portsmouth, 2m (3km)

This spur leaves the M27 at two adjacent junctions, each numbered 12, and goes down the east side of Portsmouth harbour to end at North End, a short distance from the Continental ferry port. There are no intermediate junctions.

JUNCTION at Mile End Road, Portsmouth

¼m (0.5km) S on Old Commercial Road

Charles Dickens's birthplace Small Georgian house neatly smartened up; contains a few items relating to novelist and his novels.

1m (1.5km) SW off Queen Street

Portsmouth Dockyard and **Naval Base** Principal home port of most British sailors; in dockyard, in a roofed dry dock, *Mary Rose*, flower of Henry VIII's navy, with brilliant exhibition of her history and her raising from the seabed in 1982; close by, H.M.S. *Victory*, fleet flagship at Trafalgar, a long-time and very worthwhile tourist attraction; queues must be expected in summer; oldest ironclad afloat, H.M.S. *Warrior* is due to

M27
Fareham
Southampton
(A31)
A3
Petersfield
A27
Chichester
& local roads

3½m(5.6km)

N
▲

Portsmouth
City Centre

make a third important museum-warship in 1987.

2m (3km) S via town centre on Clarence Esplanade, Southsea

Sea Life Centre, might be described as aquatic safari park; and **D-day Museum,** a stylish new museum portraying Normandy landings of 1944 in spectacular fashion.

2½m (4km) SE via Fratton
Royal Marines Museum, Eastney. History of Britain's seagoing soldiers from 1644; there were few chapters of island story in which they did *not* appear; colourful and immaculate exhibition without frills, housed in Royal Marines' centuries-old main depot.

M3: Sunbury to Winchester, 52m (83km)

The M3 begins 14m (22.5km) from central London and threads the south-western suburbs and a green and prosperous well-built-up countryside to Basingstoke. Beyond Basingstoke, views open up of the exceptionally fertile Hampshire landscape and the thickly-wooded region of Micheldever Forest, one of the most picturesque stretches of motorway in Britain. Traffic flows freely as a rule, but at the London end there is inevitably some congestion with commuter traffic morning and evening. Between Junction 3 and 5 on either side of the route are the stamping-grounds of the British Army — Aldershot, Camberley, Sandhurst, Bisley and Bagshot Heath — and convoys of military vehicles are sometimes encountered near the various training areas. This area is also a hotbed of military museums. Motorway extensions have now reached Winchester, and the M3 will eventually end on the M27 at Southampton.

JUNCTION 1

SUNBURY

1½m (2.5km) W on A308
Wrongly considered an archetype of suburbia, Sunbury is historic with several points of interest; attractive old houses includes **Flower Pot inn** and **Sunbury Court,** now a Salvation Army youth centre; **reservoir,** one of a chain, attracts multitudinous wildfowl including heron and great crested grebe;

Thorpe Park, W of town at Thorpe village, was Britain's first theme park and, additional to aquatic amusements, has replica prehistoric lake villages on its interconnecting man-made ponds.
Shepperton, S of town, has well-known film studios and an atmospheric little **town square;** when Dickens sent Bill Sikes and Oliver to rob the Shepperton house in *Oliver Twist,* they slept

under the yew tree in **St Mary's churchyard,** Lower Sunbury.

4m (6.5km) E on A308

Hampton Court Palace
Major tourist showplace, big enough to accommodate thousands; staterooms, tapestries, pictures including Mantegna cartoons and well-known royal portraits; broad parklands spread to landing-stage on Thames; maze in gardens, scene of comic incidents in J.K. Jerome's *Three Men in a Boat;* 'real' tennis court. Above park, at Teddington, **Strawberry Hill,** Horace Walpole's eccentric country house which gave its name to frothy 'Strawberry Hill Gothic' style.

1
A308 Sunbury Kingston
A316 Central London

6m(9.6km)

M25
The North (M1)
Heathrow (M4)
Staines (A30)
Chertsey (A320)
Gatwick (M23)

2
7m(11.2km) to J3

M25

M3: *3-4*

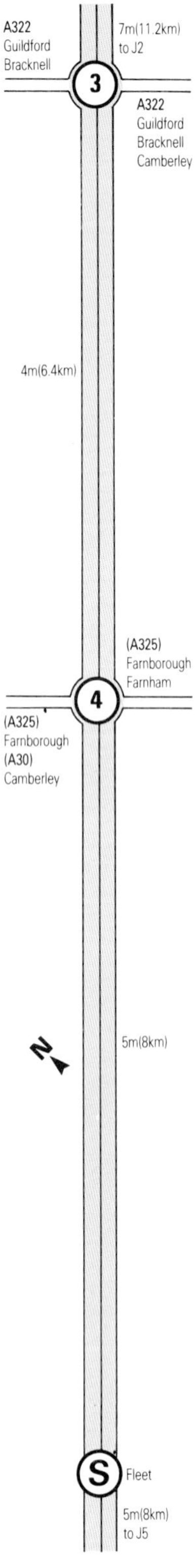
A322
Guildford
Bracknell
7m(11.2km)
to J2
3
A322
Guildford
Bracknell
Camberley
4m(6.4km)
(A325)
Farnborough
Farnham
4
(A325)
Farnborough
(A30)
Camberley
N
5m(8km)
S
Fleet
5m(8km)
to J5

JUNCTION 3

7m (11km) NE off A30
Savill and Valley Gardens See M4 Junction 5. En route, S side of Valley Gardens on N bank of Virginia Water, 100ft (30m) **totem pole** at Kurume Punchbowl of Japanese azaleas.

4m (6.5km) NW off A322
South Hill Park See A329(M) Junction A

½m (1km) S off A322
Lightwater Park Part of Bagshot Heath maintained with Countryside Commission aid as an area of natural beauty; heather, woodland, fishing, lake, bridleways.

JUNCTION 4

6m (9.5km) S on A325

Military Museum and Visitor Centre, Queens Avenue, Aldershot. Spick-and-span presentation of history of Aldershot camp and Farnborough airfield, homes of British Army and old Royal Flying Corps respectively; curious miscellanea range from Sopwith Camels to the grave of a pet lioness; detailed and fascinating tableaux of soldier's life down the centuries. Other military museums in Aldershot are **Airborne Forces,** Queens Avenue; **Royal Army Medical Corps,** Ash Vale; **Royal Army Dental Corps,** Evelyn Woods Road; **Royal Corps of Transport,** Alison Road; and **Royal Army Veterinary Corps,** Gallwey Road. For **Gurkha Museum,** see Junction 5.

9m (14.5km) S on A325
The Maltings, Farnham. On banks of Wey river, preserved and renovated complex of tannery, brewhouse, malthouse; now concert hall, leisure and arts centre; nearly always something going on; conducted tours occasional Sats am. Close by on Castle Street,

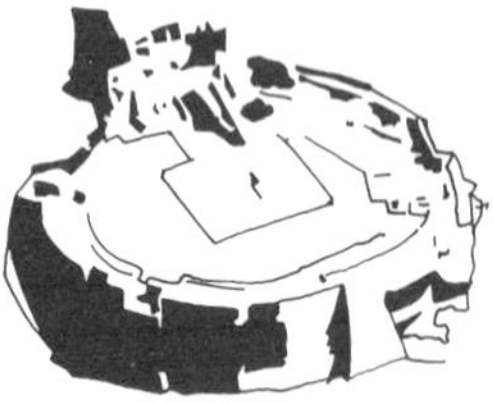

Farnham Castle, 12th-century fortress much knocked about but substantially rebuilt and modified, still inhabited; mature gardens; park noted for lawns and Lebanon cedars; keep is open daily in summer, castle on Wed. only.

JUNCTION 5

7m (11km) N on A32
Stratfield Saye and
**Wellington Country
Park.** See M4
Junction 11

ODIHAM

2m (3km) S on A287
Historic mellow-bricked
village; from ruined
castle King John set out
for his capitulation at
Runnymede; **pest house**
where plague victims
were isolated; stocks,
whipping post in
churchyard; handsome
Georgian high street;
Odiham Common, oaks
and birdlife; secluded
reaches of **Basingstoke
Canal** with shady
towpath walks and
56-seater narrow boat
trips between Odiham
and Blacksmith's
Bridge.

11m (17.5km) SE on A287
The Maltings, Farnham,
and **Farnham Castle.**
See Junction 4

*9m (14.5km) SE on A287
and B3013*

Gurkha Museum,
Church Crookham.
Memorabilia of famous
Indian regiment;
uniforms, rare medals.
Closed Sat., Sun. and
bank holidays.

JUNCTION 6

5m (8km) N off A339

The Vyne, Sherborne St
John. Beautiful Tudor

5m(8km)
to services

A32
Alton

(5)

A287
Farnham
Guildford

5m(8km)

A33
Basingstoke
Reading
Alton

(6)

5m(8km)
to J7

A33
Basingstoke
Newbury

house of diaper
brickwork; chapel;
gardens, herbaceous
borders, lake. Closed
Mon., Fri. and winter.

2m (3km) N off A33

Basing House, Old
Basing. Former
grandeur of Tudor
mansion is ruined, but
16th-century tithe barn
survives amid current
excavations; small
exhibition shows history
of site. Open Tue.,
Wed. and Fri. in
summer, occasionally
Sat. and Sun. Closed in
winter. **Tylney Hall
hotel,** Rotherwick,
Basingstoke. Majestic
country house, 37
luxurious apartments,
cordon bleu cooking;
expensive. Tel: (025 672)
4881.

*13km (21km) S on A339
near Alton*

Jane Austen's house,
Chawton. The author
lived here for last 8
years of her life,
1809-1817, and
produced her most
admired works;
300-year-old listed
building; furniture,
documents, personal
items, Jane's governess
cart; bakehouse; oak
tree planted by novelist
in 1809 still flourishes.
Closed weekdays in
winter.

JUNCTION 7

1m (1.5km) S on byroad
Dummer A pretty
village, one-time home
of the Duchess of York.

JUNCTION 8

*10m (16km) W on A303
and A34*

Silk Mill, Winchester
Street, Whitchurch.
Georgian water-mill on
River Test; unique
arrangement of power
looms and winding
gear; silk production
continues. Closed Sat.,
Sun., bank holidays.

JUNCTION 9

10m (16km) E on A31

Watercress Line,
Alresford. Restored
mid-Hants railway,
partly steam-powered,
from Alresford to Alton
(10m (16km)) through
leafy villages and good
scenery; lineside picnic
spots and country
walks; departures daily
Jul. and Aug.; daily
except Mon. May and
June; weekends only
spring and autumn;
closed winter except for
special events.

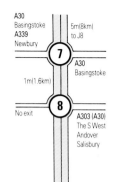

A30
Basingstoke
A339
Newbury

5m(8km)
to J8

7

A30
Basingstoke

1m(1.6km)

8

No exit

A303 (A30)
The S West
Andover
Salisbury

11m(17.6km)

A34
The Midlands
Newbury

9

A272
Winchester

1¾m(2.8km)

10

A33 (S only)

Access from
A33(N) &
A272 only

Projected

JUNCTION 10

WINCHESTER
1m (1.5km) SW on A33.

Ancient capital and seat
of kings; 11th-century
cathedral replaced hoary
Saxon minster; oldest
crypt in existence;
serene and tranquil
close with half-timbered
houses of great
antiquity; **Winchester
College,** among oldest
public schools, open
daily, guided tours in
summer; **Great Hall** (c.
1225) has legendary

Round Table of King
Arthur; **City Museum
and Heritage Centre,**
Upper Brook Street,
give historical rundown
of 1000 years;
archaeological digs in
progress under **Castle,
St Mary's Abbey** and
cathedral close; lovely
Abbey Gardens, at foot
of Eastgate behind King
Alfred's statue,
incorporate delightful
children's garden and
aromatic garden for the
blind; interesting walks
include **The Weirs**
(follow River Itchen
from City Bridge),
Watermeadows (follow
signposts from College
Street to St Cross) and
St Giles Hill for
splendid panorama of
city (gentle climb from
Broadway). **Mr Pitkin's
eating-house and wine
bar,** 4 Jewry Street; not
too elegant, but good
cooking, varied menus
and quite cheap.
Tel: (0962) 55525.

M32:

Winterbourne to Bristol, 4½m (7km)

The Bristol Parkway leaves the M4 at Junction 19 and its terminal junction (3) comes to within 1m (1.5km) of the city centre.

JUNCTION 1

7m (11km) E on B4465

Dyrham Park Mellow Bath stone house of dignified appearance with a monumental facade, set on wooded slope; original (William and Mary) panelling and hangings; ancient trees in deer park; waterfowl; picnickers welcome; a worthwhile great house not overrun by visitors. Park open daily, house closed Fri. and in winter.

JUNCTION 3

BRISTOL

1m (1.5km) S on Newfoundland Road
Important western ocean seaport from far back, heavily involved with tobacco, sugar, slave and sherry trade, with privateering and American exploration; **St Mary Redcliffe** church with soaring spire, 'fairest parish church in England', said Good Queen Bess; **Christmas Steps,** steep flight with little old shops selling curios and antiques;

SS Great Britain, one-funnelled,

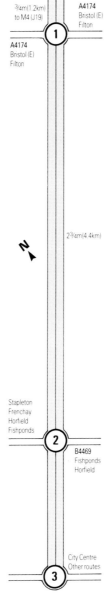

six-masted, first ocean-going, screw-driven iron ship in history, now 145 years old, at Great Western Dock off Cumberland Road, video of restoration and a snack bar on board; **Watershed** quayside shopping/restaurant complex off Canons Road;

Clifton Zoo, small, old-established, with interesting nocturnal house and lovely gardens; adjoining Zoo, **Clifton Down,** pleasant walks; below, across **Avon Gorge,**

Brunel's famous **suspension bridge** of 1864; on Brandon Hill, **Cabot Tower** commemorating the old Bristol seadog's discovery of continental America, panoramic views of city. The air-raids of 1940-41 destroyed Bristol's ancient heart and of city gates only **St John's,** foot of Broad Street, survives. **Harvey's restaurant,** Denmark Street, prestigious eating-house in well-known sherry-importers' wine cellar, with wine museum adjoining. Tel: (0272) 277665

Map labels:
¾m(1.2km) to M4 (J19)
A4174 Bristol (E) Filton
A4174 Bristol (E) Filton
N
2¾m(4.4km)
Stapleton Frenchay Horfield Fishponds
B4469 Fishponds Horfield
City Centre Other routes
① ② ③

A3(M):

Horndean to Langstone, 5m (8km)

This short section of trunk-road motorway descends from the rolling well-timbered landscape of the South Downs to the muddy creeks and inlets of the coast near the terminus of the M27, with which it will one day be connected. Already, as part of the main highway between London and Portsmouth and the Isle of Wight ferries, it is a busy route in summer. The junctions are temporarily lettered A to E.

JUNCTION A

4½m (7km) N on A3
Queen Elizabeth Country Park 500 acres (200 hectares) of wooded hillside with footpaths, bridle paths and good views towards the coast; grass ski-ing; reconstructed primitive village and Iron Age farm at Butser Hill.
Sussex Border Path, long-distance walk from Rowland's Castle to East Grinstead, passes across E side of park.

JUNCTION B

3m (5km) E on B2149
Rowland's Castle Not a castle in sight, but **Red Hill** has 'invasion rooms' occupied by war leaders at Normandy landings; easy 2m (3km) walk through forest leads to

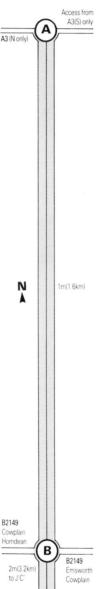

Stanstead Park (Earl of Bessborough), elegant Georgian house with tapestries, porcelain, notable collection of bird paintings of various eras;

Regency Gothic chapel; walled gardens (produce sold in shop); full upstairs-downstairs tour of house; small museum of theatrical costumes; cricket on lawns (summer Suns., weather permitting); house also accessible by car via Rowland's Castle or Westbourne. Closed Wed.-Sat. and all winter.

Access from A3(S) only

(A) A3 (N only)

N ▲

1m(1.6km)

B2149 Cowplain Horndean

(B)

2m(3.2km) to J'C'

B2149 Emsworth Cowplain

JUNCTION C

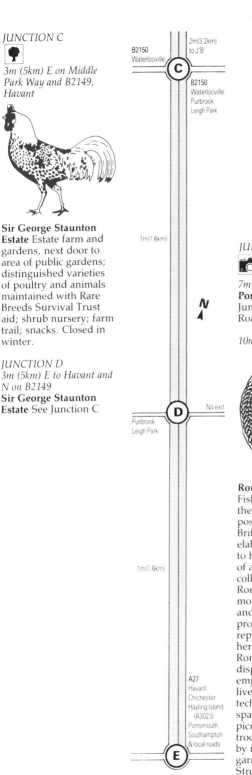

3m (5km) E on Middle Park Way and B2149, Havant

Sir George Staunton Estate Estate farm and gardens, next door to area of public gardens; distinguished varieties of poultry and animals maintained with Rare Breeds Survival Trust aid; shrub nursery; farm trail; snacks. Closed in winter.

JUNCTION D
3m (5km) E to Havant and N on B2149
Sir George Staunton Estate See Junction C

B2150
Waterlooville

2m(3.2km)
to J'B'

C

B2150
Waterlooville
Purbrook
Leigh Park

1m(1.6km)

N

D   No exit

Purbrook
Leigh Park

1m(1.6km)

A27
Havant
Chichester
Hayling Island
(A3023)
Portsmouth
Southampton
& local roads

E

JUNCTION E

7m (12km) W on A27
Portsmouth See M275 Junction (-) at Mile End Road

10m (16km) E on A27

Roman Palace, Fishbourne. Probably the most exciting post-1945 discovery in British archaeology; elaborate villa thought to have been residence of a British king, a collaborator with Romans; intricate floor mosaics; baths; museum and audio-visual programme; garden replanted with archaic herbs according to Roman plan; farming displays in summer, employing Roman-type livestock and cultivation techniques; cafeteria; spacious and attractive picnic area; occasional trooping the colour etc. by resident, 'Roman' garrison, the Ermine Street Guard. Closed weekdays in Dec., Jan. and Feb.

A329 (M):

Bracknell to Reading, 7m (11km)

The function of this isolated (M) highway, crossing the M4 at Junction 10, will become clearer as it extends eastward to the M25 (London ring motorway) and westward to the M40 (London-Oxford motorway). At present it serves only Reading and is a fairly quiet road, useful as a diversion when the M4 is trafficbound. Its junctions bear the provisional symbols A, B and C.

JUNCTION A

2m (3km) SE off A329

South Hill Park
Ambitious arts centre in and around Georgian house and park, with year-round programme of theatre, music and exhibitions. In immediate neighbourhood are **Crowthorne Wood** (a noteworthy sequoia avenue at Wick Hill) and Bagshot Road **picnic area.**

JUNCTION B

2m (3km) N on A321
Deep fords, a rarity nowadays in Britain, on byroad which crosses Loddon river between Twyford and Sonning.

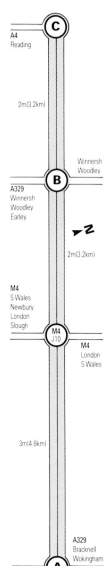

C
A4
Reading

2m(3.2km)

Winnersh
Woodley

B
A329
Winnersh
Woodley
Earley

2m(3.2km)

M4
S Wales
Newbury
London
Slough

M4
J10

M4
London
S Wales

3m(4.8km)

A329
Bracknell
Wokingham

A

JUNCTION C

2m (3km) W on A4

English Rural Life Museum, Reading, S on Aldershot road A327. Important national collection of craft and domestic items; shows in scholarly detail the progress of English agriculture from earliest times; also Greek pottery exhibition.

A308 (M):

M4 to Maidenhead east, ½m (1km)

A423 (M):

M4 to Maidenhead west, 2m (3km)

These 2 short spurs off the M4 at Junctions 8/9 lead into roads for Maidenhead town centre, Boulter's Lock and Cookham Dene; and to the town's west end and the A423 road to Oxford. There is no intermediate junction on the A308(M). The 2 junctions on the A423(M) are provisionally numbered 9A and 9B.

JUNCTION (-)

📷 🌳 **H** 🍴 🏛

A308(M)
MAIDENHEAD
1½m (2km) N
Thames-side home of numerous show-business personalities; river trips and regattas;

Boulter's Lock, Cookham Lock, Bridge Gardens, Guards Club Island, fine 18th-century **road bridge** and nearby

A308(M)

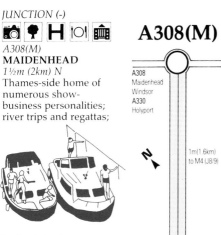

A308
Maidenhead
Windsor
A330
Holyport

1m(1.6km)
to M4 (J8/9)

A423(M)

9b

A4
Reading
Maidenhead
A423
Henley
(A404)

2m(3.2km)

9a
Local roads   Local roads

1m(1.6km)
to M4 (J8/9)

Skindles, a hotel associated with indiscretions of pre-Victorian royalty. Tel: (0628) 23366.
Waterside Inn, Bray; charming setting, superior cuisine, essential to book. Tel: (0628) 20691.

4m (6.5km) N on A4094
Stanley Spencer Gallery, Cookham Dene. Small but absorbing collection of paintings by Cookham's eccentric genius.

JUNCTION 9B A423(M)
1m (1.5km) W on A4

Shire Horse Centre, Cherry Garden Lane. Brewery company's exhibition of heavy horses, drays, harnesses, brasses; tearoom and picnic area; closed in winter.

M4: London to Pont Abraham, including A48(M) the Cardiff Spur, 200m (320km)

Nearly 50 junctions mark the course of this motorway between London's Chiswick flyover and the mountains of West Wales. The first part of the route is that of the old Great West Road, following the valleys of Thames and Kennet and curving round the Vale of the White Horse and the Cotswolds — an open, civilized landscape. Among several engineering triumphs is the Severn Bridge, which carries the M4 into Wales. A number of large industrial towns — Newport, Cardiff, Port Talbot, Neath, Swansea — are closely bypassed. Spurs take traffic into the off-lying towns of Maidenhead (see A308(M)) and A423(M)), Reading (see A329(M)), Bristol (see M32) and Cardiff. The Welsh section of the route is driven through some delightfully varied and hilly scenery and it will eventually be extended to the Pembrokeshire coast. M4 congestion on the London approach is notorious; there is often a build-up of traffic in Wales too, where the 3-lane carriageway is in places reduced to 2 lanes.

JUNCTION 1
Access to central **London** (Hyde Park Corner 4m (6.5km))

JUNCTION 2
🌳 🏛 🍽 📷

2m (3km) SW off A4

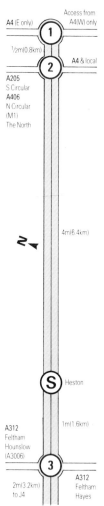

Syon House, Brentford. Spacious park sloping to Thames with lake, water-lilies, prolific rose-gardens; house (Duke of Northumberland) open to public; pioneer garden centre (1968); motor-car museum, motor-racing broadcasts; butterfly house, mostly occupied with souvenir shop; good cafeteria, inexpensive restaurant.

KEW
3m (5km) S on A30
Village with green; **churchyard** where some celebrities are buried; small **royal palace,** open in summer, glimpse of private life of George III; world-famous **Botanical Gardens,** vast diversity of plants and trees;

[Map diagram:]
Access from A4(W) only
A4 (E only) — (1)
½m (0.8km)
(2) — A4 & local
A205 S Circular
A406 N Circular (M1) The North
4m (6.4km)
(S) Heston
1m (1.6km)
A312 Feltham Hounslow (A3006)
(3) — A312 Feltham Hayes
2m (3.2km) to J4

pagoda, slender piece of chinoiserie.

RICHMOND
5m (8km) S on A30
Beautiful terraced houses round Green and on Richmond Hill, associated with 17th/18th-century courtiers, politicians, actresses; many trendy shops and coffee bars, quite a Continental air; 18th-century delicacy, 'maids of honour' (small light cheesecakes), made exclusively to secret recipe at **Newens Cake Shop,** Kew Road; **deer park,** largest of royal parks, with ponds, fine trees and deer roaming in search of generous picnickers; across river on Kew Bridge Road, majestic steam engines of a bygone era at **Pumping and Water Supply Museum** (weekends only); next door, a **Musical Museum.**

JUNCTION 4

1½m (2.5km) S on airport spur to Junction 4A
Heathrow Airport
World's busiest; rooftop viewing terrace. **Petit Four restaurant,** Terminal 4, opened 1986; sub-tropical décor; valiant effort to counteract bad image of airport food and service, successful so far; fairly expensive.

JUNCTION 5

RUNNYMEDE
4½m (7km) S via Datchet off B376
From riverbank meads (A308 W of roundabout) **Magna Carta Island** (private) is visible; Lutyens stone kiosks and memorial buildings; **Commonwealth Air Force Cloister Memorial,** simple yet striking, on Cooper's Hill; **Magna Carta Memorial** (put up by American lawyers) and **Kennedy Memorial** (1965) on riverbank; **Englefield Green,** 1m (1.5km) S, elegant Victorian and modern houses;

also superb **Savill** and **Valley** gardens, complete horticultural range from tiny alpines to tall redwoods; not to be missed; car entrance Wick Road, Englefield Green (pay barrier); Savill closed in winter.

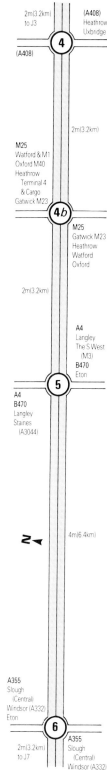

2m(3.2km) to J3

(A408) Heathrow Uxbridge

(4)

(A408)

2m(3.2km)

M25 Watford & M1 Oxford M40 Heathrow Terminal 4 & Cargo Gatwick M23

(4b)

M25 Gatwick M23 Heathrow Watford Oxford

2m(3.2km)

A4 Langley The S West (M3) B470 Eton

(5)

A4 B470 Langley Staines (A3044)

4m(6.4km)

A355 Slough (Central) Windsor (A332) Eton

(6)

2m(3.2km) to J7

A355 Slough (Central) Windsor (A332)

JUNCTION 6

ETON
3m (5km) S on B3022

College, Chapel and **Museum of Eton Life** open daily Apr.-Sept. except certain special days; from College, High Street descends to Thames with old-world shops, Georgian buildings, unique Victorian pillar-box, punishment stocks outside Cockpit; **Eton Bridge,** all-pedestrian, viewpoint for College boating; from bridge, a short walk to **Windsor Castle** (see below). **House on the Bridge restaurant,** former boathouse, excellent *à la carte,* serves late suppers, expensive but has also good **Eton Buttery,** cheaper. Tel: (01) 95 60914.

WINDSOR
1½m (2.5km) S on A355 and A332

Best take guided tour of **Castle,** which includes St George's Chapel, Horseshoe Cloister, Albert Memorial Chapel and Windsor old town and guildhall and daily pageantry. At town railway station, **Royalty and Empire Waxworks** (Tussaud's), lavish tableaux of 1897 Jubilee; **river trips** from Thames Side landing stage near footbridge to Eton; S on B3022, **Windsor Safari Park,** well-stocked, well-managed but marred by circus tricks; newly added (1986) are tropical and butterfly house, bear park and Noah's Ark playground.

M4: 7-13

2m (3km) N, W and S (recrossing motorway) on B3026

Dorney Court Neat array of Tudor gables and pink brick chimneys in topiary garden; first pineapple in England grown here, 1661; bright little **church** of St James next door; home-made cream teas and Dorney honey at house; closed Wed.-Sat. and all winter.

6m (9.5km) N via Taplow on B476
Cliveden Renowned Italianate house (formerly Lord Astor) where power politics were played; parterres and hanging woods on low cliffs above Thames; grounds open daily except Jan. and Feb.

JUNCTION 11

1½m (2.5km) NE off A33
English Rural Life Museum, Reading. See A329(M) Junction C

6m (10km) S on A33
National Dairy Museum, Stratfield Saye. Milk and cheese production through the ages; deer park and country park adjoining,

all part of **Stratfield Saye** (Duke of Wellington), imposing 17th-century country house with Iron Duke memorabilia. House closed Fri., house and park closed weekdays in winter.

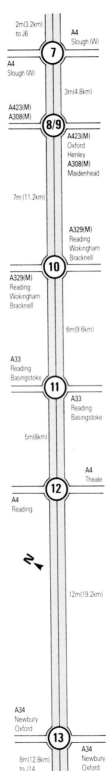

2m(3.2km)
to J6

A4
Slough (W)

7

A4
Slough (W)

3m(4.8km)

A423(M)
A308(M)

8/9

A423(M)
Oxford
Henley
A308(M)
Maidenhead

7m(11.2km)

A329(M)
Reading
Wokingham
Bracknell

10

A329(M)
Reading
Wokingham
Bracknell

6m(9.6km)

A33
Reading
Basingstoke

11

A33
Reading
Basingstoke

5m(8km)

A4
Theale

12

A4
Reading

12m(19.2km)

A34
Newbury
Oxford

13

A34
Newbury
Oxford

8m(12.8km)
to J14

JUNCTION 12

MAPLEDURHAM
7m (11km) N on A340 via Pangbourne or A4074 via Reading, or by boat (summer only) from Caversham Bridge hotel, Reading.
Neat old-fashioned village; country park

behind **Mapledurham House** (house is rather tame); country teas in **Old Manor;** restored working **water-mill** on Thames, sells stoneground flour. House open Sat., Sun. and public holidays, closed in winter.

JUNCTION 13

4m (6.5km) S on A34

Kennet and Avon Canal, Newbury. Motor barges ply this attractive canal, 3hr trip from Newbury Wharf, Sun. and bank holidays in summer; horsedrawn barges run 1½hr trips from Kintbury Wharf, 5m (8km) W of Newbury off A4, irregular timings, book in advance through Kennet Horse Boat Company. **Elcot Park hotel,** off A4 near Newbury, peaceful and relaxing; its Regency restaurant offers superior cuisine and vintage wines; expensive. Tel: (0488) 58100.

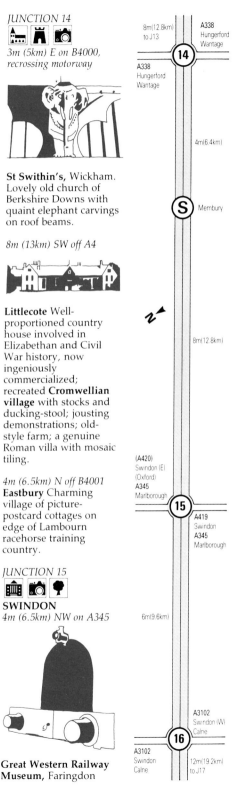

JUNCTION 14

3m (5km) E on B4000, recrossing motorway

St Swithin's, Wickham. Lovely old church of Berkshire Downs with quaint elephant carvings on roof beams.

8m (13km) SW off A4

Littlecote Well-proportioned country house involved in Elizabethan and Civil War history, now ingeniously commercialized; recreated **Cromwellian village** with stocks and ducking-stool; jousting demonstrations; old-style farm; a genuine Roman villa with mosaic tiling.

4m (6.5km) N off B4001
Eastbury Charming village of picture-postcard cottages on edge of Lambourn racehorse training country.

JUNCTION 15

SWINDON
4m (6.5km) NW on A345

Great Western Railway Museum, Faringdon

Road. Originally a railwaymen's lodging-house, now houses locomotives, models and prints; gallery portrays life and work of G.W.R.'s famous engineer, I.K. Brunel; **railway village museum** next door has typical Victorian working-class interior.

Oasis Leisure Centre, North Star Avenue. Beneath a surrealist dome, an expensively-equipped modern sports centre; lagoon swimming pool under tropical vegetation; outdoor games; cafeteria. **Coate Water Country Park,** S of town centre. Lake, birdlife, enormous sand-pit for children; agricultural museum; walks, picnic spots, barbecue hearths.

JUNCTION 16

4m (6.5km) NE on A3102
Swindon See Junction 15

2m (3km) N off A3102
Lydiard Country Park, Lydiard Tregoze. Wide and generally peaceful park and farmland near ancient **manor-house** of Lydiard and small **parish church** of St Mary's; extravagant family memorials.

67

M4: *17-18*

JUNCTION 17

CASTLE COMBE
9m (14.5km) SW on B4039

Mellow stone village, epitome of rural England; 15th-century canopied **market cross;** historic **bridge** on By Brook. **Castle hotel,** 9 rooms, updated medieval hostelry; reputable restaurant, not very roomy; moderate charges. Tel: (0249) 782461.

CORSHAM
9m (14.5km) SW off A429

Another delightful, Wiltshire village; **Corsham Court** (Lord Methuen) has paintings and furnishings appropriate to home of a renowned collector; **park** was laid out by Capability Brown, Closed Mon. and Fri. Local quarry is now **Bath Stone Quarry Museum,** living display of traditional industry.

LACOCK
8m (13km) S on A350
Another contender for title of Britain's most beautiful village; **Fox-Talbot Museum of Photography,** in barn at **Lacock Abbey,** commemorates 19th-century Lacockian who allegedly invented the camera.

12m(19.2km) to J16

A429 Cirencester Chippenham

17

A429 Cirencester Chippenham

2m(3.2km)

S

Leigh Delamere

9m(14.4km)

A46 Bath Stroud

18

A46 Bath Stroud

7m(11.2km)

M32 Bristol

19

M32 Bristol

3m(4.8km) to J20

JUNCTION 18

2m (3km) S on A46
Dyrham Park See M32 Junction 1

BATH
9m (14.5km) S on A46

Outstanding Regency architecture and evocative Roman remains. City full of well-publicized, first-rate attractions. An unusual one is **Monkton Farleigh Mine,** Bathford, underground ammunition dump of World War II, brilliantly maintained (closed winter weekdays). Also **Bath Postal Museum,** on site of first penny-post office; and the

American Museum at Claverton Manor, a compendium of Americana — covered waggons, Indian culture and warfare, Spanish missions, religious minorities, kitchenware, beehive ovens, 19th-century 'parlors'.

JUNCTION 21

½m (1km) W
Severn Road Bridge
One of the newer
estuary bridges (toll),
2½m (4km) long,
already carrying heavier
traffic than envisaged;
free footway offers
broad views up and
down Bristol Channel.

1½m (2.5km) SW off A403
Fossil Beach, on byroad
from Aust, combed by
amateur geologists.

JUNCTION 22

CHEPSTOW
2m (3km) N on A466

Medieval town of
narrow streets, girdled
with walls above muddy
Wye estuary; sombre
relic of **Norman castle,**
first stonebuilt fortress
in Britain; **Gate
Museum** exposes rich
heritage of Border
citadel (closed in
winter). **Castle View
hotel,** adjoining Gate; 8
comfortable rooms,
better-than-average
cuisine, not expensive.
Tel: (029 12) 70349

5m (8km) N on A466

Tintern Abbey Graceful
12th-century pillars and
arches in picturesque
riverside setting;
exhibition on life of
Cistercian monks. **Old
Station** nearby offers
'picnic on the platform'
plus walks and railway
exhibition.

7m (11km) NW on A466,

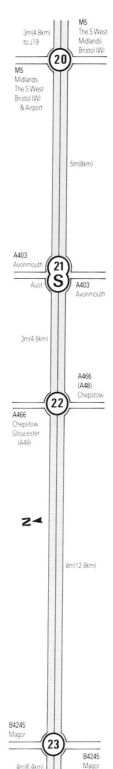

*3m(4.8km)
to J19*

M5
The S West
Midlands
Bristol (W)

20

M5
Midlands
The S West
Bristol (W)
& Airport

5m(8km)

A403
Avonmouth

21 S

Aust | A403
Avonmouth

3m(4.8km)

A466
(A48)
Chepstow

22

A466
Chepstow
Gloucester
(A48)

8m(12.8km)

B4245
Magor

23

*4m(6.4km)
to J24* | B4245
Magor

*B4293 and unclassified
roads*

Model Farm Museum,
Wolves Newton.
Lifesized farmhouse,
barn and waggonshed
display techniques of
rural architecture;
museum has Victorian
room, naughty postcard
room, domestic bric-à-
brac, toys; craftshop,
café. Closed in winter.

JUNCTION 23

4½m (7km) SE on B4245
Caldicot Castle Great
Hall of partly-ruined
fortress has medieval
banquets nightly, done
with more flair than
most; tower gallery has
crafts exhibitions; small
museum boasts relics
from Nelson's flagship
H.M.S. *Foudroyant.* Tel:
(0291) 420241

M4: *24-28*

JUNCTION 24

5m (8km) E on A48

Penhow Castle
Picturesque fortified
mansion, said to be
oldest inhabited house
in Wales (c. 1150); still
lived in; visitors
agreeably
unregimented;
eminently visitable.

3m (5km) NW on B4236

Caerleon Large Roman
station with
amphitheatre, barracks,
shops, baths, temples
spread under modern
town; some interesting
restorations; in town
centre, **Legionary
Museum. Kemeys
Manor restaurant;** offers
'Taste of Wales' cuisine.
Tel: (063 349) 380

7m (11km) N on A449
**Mr Midgeley's
restaurant,** Usk;
sophisticated cooking,
carefully-chosen wines,
predominantly French
flavour; not too
expensive.

JUNCTION 25
2m (3km) NE off B4596
Caerleon See Junction
24

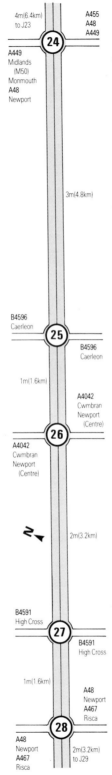

4m(6.4km)
to J23

A455
A48
A449

24

A449
Midlands
(M50)
Monmouth
A48
Newport

3m(4.8km)

B4596
Caerleon

25

B4596
Caerleon

1m(1.6km)

A4042
Cwmbran
Newport
(Centre)

26

A4042
Cwmbran
Newport
(Centre)

2m(3.2km)

B4591
High Cross

27

B4591
High Cross

1m(1.6km)

A48
Newport
A467
Risca

28

A48
Newport
A467
Risca

2m(3.2km)
to J29

JUNCTION 26

NEWPORT
1m (1.5km) S on A4042
Commercial town and
popular shopping
centre; small **St Woolos
Cathedral** sinking under
massive Norman arch;
renowned **Feibusch
murals** in civic centre
portray borough's
history from Celtic
times.

JUNCTION 27

1m (1.5km) NW off B4591
Monmouthshire Canal
14 locks rise is a novelty
for canal buffs; a rather
dilapidated scene for
others, but there are
towpath walks, a picnic
area and visitor centre.

JUNCTION 28

2m (3km) E off A48
Transporter Bridge,
Newport Docks.
Technicological wonder
of Edwardian
engineering.

½m (1km) S on A48

**Tredegar House and
Country Park** Plain but
well-proportioned 17th-
century country house
in 90 acres (36 hectares)
of lily-fringed lake and
dense woodland; bird
garden; craft
workshops; a pleasant
layout, but overcrowded
at holiday times. House
closed Mon. and
sometimes Tue.

JUNCTION 29

CARDIFF
9m (14.5km) SW on A48(M) and A48
Fine white classical complex of Welsh Office, Law Courts, City Hall, University etc. dignifies an otherwise shabby conurbation; domed **Museum of Wales** historically interesting for sculpted stones and crosses; in Bute Street, dockland, **Industrial and Maritime Museum** summarizes Welsh mining, steelworking, shipbuilding and civil engineering history;

open-air **Welsh Folk Museum,** St Fagan's, W of centre, has reconstructed cottages, mills, costume exhibitions, traditional crafts; restaurant.

JUNCTION 32

5m (8km) SE on A470
Cardiff See Junction 29

2m (3km) NW off A470

Castell Coch 'Red Castle', pseudo-baronial

Victorian extravaganza; fanciful décor depicts exotic fauna and scenes from Aesop; **museum** tells of Lord Bute, shipowner, eccentric, the castle's creator; original architect's drawings well displayed; picnic in tranquil wooded area round castle.

6m (9.5km) N on A470 and B4600
Caerphilly Castle
'Sleeping giant of Welsh castles' — stark crumbling ruin occupying 30 acres (12 hectares) inside formidable concentric rings of defences; Great Hall made habitable without losing character. Closed in winter.

JUNCTION 33

3m (5km) S on A4232
Welsh Folk Museum, St Fagan's. See **Cardiff** Junction 29.

5m (8km) S on A4232 and W on A48

Dyffryn Gardens, St Nicholas. Somewhat municipal park atmosphere, but undeniably impressive sheltered gardens with formal flower-beds, desert and tropical plant houses and broad immaculate lawns; arboreta with early-flowering shrubs; tearoom and garden shop; former home of millionaire shipowning Cory family. Open Apr.-Sept. and weekends in Oct.

2m(3.2km) to J28

A48(M) Cardiff

29

No exit

3m(4.8km)

Projected

30

Projected

3m(4.8km)

N

Projected

31

Projected

2m(3.2km)

A470 Cardiff Merthyr Tydfil

32

A470 Merthyr Tydfil Cardiff

3m(4.8km)

A4232 Cardiff (W) Barry Penarth Cardiff Airport

33

A4232 Cardiff Barry

3m(4.8km) to J34

M4: 34-38

JUNCTION 34

5m (8km) S on unclassified road to A48
Dyffryn Gardens See Junction 33

6m (9.5km) SW on A4119, A4222 and A48
Cowbridge Market town, walled and gated; good picnicking in **Tair Onen larchwoods,** overlooking 12th-century **parish church** of Welsh St Donats; promising **Roman excavations** hereabouts; off Cowbridge High Street, **Woolbarn** craft workshops.

JUNCTION 35

5m (8km) SW via Bridgend on B4265
Ewenny Historic community with **Norman priory** and long-established **potteries;** café, showroom. Closed in winter.

JUNCTION 36

4m (6.5km) N on A4061 and/or A4064
Here begin scenic drives of 10-20m (16-32km) on tortuous roads through **Ogmore forests** and **Garw valleys;** new

country park at Bryngarw, off A4065, round a pretty house and fascinating but rather moist wild garden.

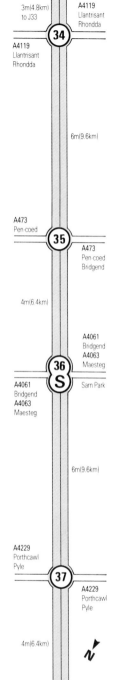

3m(4.8km) to J33 — A4119 Llantrisant Rhondda

34

A4119 Llantrisant Rhondda

6m(9.6km)

A473 Pen-coed — **35** — A473 Pen-coed Bridgend

4m(6.4km)

A4061 Bridgend A4063 Maesteg — **36 S** — Sarn Park

A4061 Bridgend A4063 Maesteg

6m(9.6km)

A4229 Porthcawl Pyle — **37** — A4229 Porthcawl Pyle

4m(6.4km)

A48 Port Talbot — **38** — A48 Port Talbot

A48 Port Talbot

3m(4.8km) to J40

JUNCTION 37

3m (5km) S via Porthcawl on B4238
Access to **Heritage Coast, Margam Sands** and **Kenfig Pool.** See Junction 38

JUNCTION 38

3m (5km) W on sandy tracks via Kenfig
Heritage Coast Sandy extremity of string of beaches and headlands which begins E near Barry; **Kenfig Pool** popular with picnickers, newly-created **Dunes nature reserve** round it is of ornithological interest; **Margam Sands** and **'Burrows'** 2m (3km) N of Pool are a long and generally unfrequented stretch of beach and dunes.

½m (1km) E off A48

Margam Abbey Cathedral-like mansion; in gardens, the biggest orangery in Wales and the open-air Welsh Sculpture Park;

signposted walks across open parkland with lake and deer; film theatre, travelogues of locality. Closed Mon. in summer, Mon. and Tue. in winter.

JUNCTION 40

🌳 🏛️

7m (12km) NE on A4107

Afan Argoed,
Cynonville. Country
park near head of
Valleys, under high bare
hills; birdlife; Welsh

Miners Museum
displays primitive
equipment and portrays
child labour of bad old
days. Museum closed in
winter.

3m(4.8km) to J38

A4107 Port Talbot

40

A4107 Port Talbot

1m(1.6km)

A48 Port Talbot

41

No exit

2m(3.2km)

A48 Swansea

Temporary terminal

A48 Swansea (E)

44

2m(3.2km) to J45

JUNCTION 41
8m (13km) NE on B4486 and A4107
Afan Argoed See Junction 40

(M4 ends 2m (3km) beyond Junction 41 and begins again with partly-completed Junction 44)

JUNCTION 44

🏘️ 📷 🌳

5m (8km) E on A465
Neath Abbey Religion and industry join hands in these extensive 13th-century Cistercian ruins, where primitive iron and copper smelting was carried on; fine undercroft (crypt).

7m (11km) NE via Neath, off A465
Penscynor Wildlife Park, Cilfrew. About 350 species of birds and animals; tropical fish; chairlift and Alpine Slide; cafeteria; nearby are **Aberdulais Falls** (National Trust) on Dulais river, with ancient metal workings in the gorge; also **canal junction** in Aberdulais village, where two canals and two rivers come together in the shadows of a great aqueduct and an unusual skew bridge.

73

M4: 45-49

JUNCTION 45

SWANSEA
4m (6.5km) S on A4067
Once a grimy coal and steel port, now ambitiously face-lifted; huge **market hall** packed with honey, cheese, seafood and miscellaneous stalls; custom-built **Maritime Quarter** has 'waterfront village' with theatres, restaurants, art gallery and sailing schools; **Taliesin Gallery** at University College has contemporary Welsh art; on W side of town, **Clyne Country Park,** walks and cycle track on disused railway; **Drangway restaurant,** Wind Street, Swansea; 'Taste of Wales' and of France too; moderate prices. Tel: (0792) 461397.
W along seafront (4m

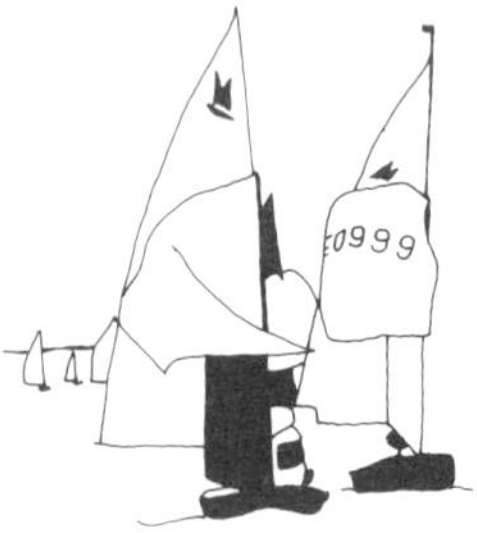

(7km)) **Mumbles** with pier, Norman castle, cafés, fine coastal walks to W round inlets clothed in greenery; rock pools.

12m (19km) NE on A4067

Dan-yr-Ogof Caves A labyrinth, including the

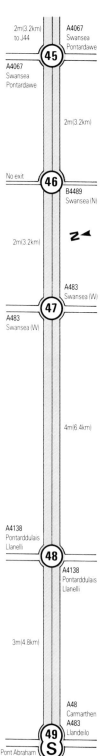

longest and loftiest showcaves in Britain; dinosaur precinct; archaeological museum. Closed in winter.

JUNCTION 46
5m (8km) S on B4489
Swansea See Junction 45

JUNCTION 47
6m (9.5km) S on A483
Swansea. See Junction 45. Best route to **Mumbles.**

JUNCTION 49

15m (24km) N on A483
Dinefwr Castle, Llandeilo. Once the greatest of strongholds of the Welsh princes, dramatic in decay in its commanding situation; under restoration, rarely open to public, but a fine sight at close range; nature reserve in surrounding Castle Woods may be entered.

7m (11km) N on A483
The Cobblers restaurant, Church Street, Llandybie, has won prizes for excellence of country-based cuisine; not expensive. Tel: (0269) 850540.

Map labels (northbound):
- 2m(3.2km) to J44
- A4067 Swansea Pontardawe
- **45**
- A4067 Swansea Pontardawe
- 2m(3.2km)
- No exit
- **46**
- B4489 Swansea (N)
- 2m(3.2km)
- A483 Swansea (W)
- **47**
- A483 Swansea (W)
- 4m(6.4km)
- A4138 Pontarddulais Llanelli
- **48**
- A4138 Pontarddulais Llanelli
- 3m(4.8km)
- A48 Carmarthen A483 Llandeilo
- **49 S**
- Pont Abraham

M40: Uxbridge
to Milton Common, 31m (49km)

The M40 accompanies an historic route out of London, the A40 Oxford and Gloucester highway. It will eventually join the M5 but at present stops short of Oxford. As part of the well-known tourist triangle for foreign visitors — London, Oxford, Stratford-upon-Avon — it can be busy with touring coaches in the season. Junction 1 is 12m (19km) from central London. Soon after that the M40 disentangles itself from the suburbs and begins to wind, rise and dip across the pleasant chalk country of the Chilterns. At its highest point it reaches about 750ft (230m) and for several miles it offers a shifting kaleidoscope of pleasant pastures, woods and villages.

Three detached sections of what will one day be motorways are associated with the M40; since they are comparatively insignificant lengths, we mention them here but do not describe them separately. Two are inner-London links; West Way, A40(M), a 2½m (4km) route from Paddington to North Kensington; and the adjacent West Cross, M41, a 1m (1.5km) route connecting North Kensington with Shepherd's Bush. The third is some distance away at the northern end of the Chiltern hills. It is the A41(M), a 2½m (4km) loop on the A41 London-Aylesbury road and a bypass for Tring.

JUNCTION 1

1½m (2.5km) E on A40
Swakeleys, Ickenham. Attractive H-shaped Jacobean mansion, noted for period furnishings and stuccowork.

JUNCTION 2

2½m (4km) N off A40

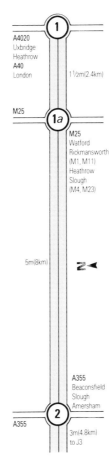

A4020
Uxbridge
Heathrow
A40
London

1½m(2.4km)

M25

M25
Watford
Rickmansworth
(M1, M11)
Heathrow
Slough
(M4, M23)

5m(8km)

A355
Beaconsfield
Slough
Amersham

A355

3m(4.8km)
to J3

Old Jordans 17th-century farmhouse revered in Society of Friends history as first Quaker meeting-place and scene of persecutions; guest-house, refectory and Mayflower Barn are set in old-world garden surrounded by beech woods; inexpensive but perfectly adequate. Tel: (02407) 45860.

2½m (4km) N via Beaconsfield off A355
Bekonscot World's

oldest model village; amazing attention to detail (artist-designed stained glass in toy church, for example); an elaborate model railway; proceeds to charity. Closed Nov.-Feb.

4m (6.5km) N off A413

Milton's Cottage, Chalfont St Giles. Picturesque 16th-century cottage and charming garden where Milton lived from 1665 and wrote *Paradise Lost*; museum of priceless relics; commemorative festival with *son et lumière* in June 1987. Closed Nov.-Jan.

75

JUNCTION 3

2½m (4km) S on A4094.
'Fawlty Towers',
Wooburn. Actually
Foxy's a downmarket
country club; non-
members may view
exterior of establishment
made famous in TV
comedy series.

4m (6.5km) S on A4094
**Stanley Spencer
Gallery,** Cookham. See
A308(M)

JUNCTION 4

HIGH WYCOMBE
2m (3km) N on A404
Many historic buildings
and plaques in nucleus
of venerable market
town; **walk** through
conservation area
outlined in leaflet
obtainable at tourist

office; **Wycombe Chair
Museum,** Priory
Avenue, shows
development of famous
'Windsor' chair and
other traditional

3m(4.8km)
to J2

A40
Wycombe (E)

3

No exit

4m(6.4km)

A404
Wycombe
Marlow
Maidenhead
(M4)

4

A404
Wycombe
Marlow

8m(12.8km)
to J5

---

patterns. Closed Wed.,
Sun. and bank holidays.

3m (5km) N on A4010
The Caves, West
Wycombe.
Overshadowed by their
notoriety as *Hell-Fire
Club* venue in 1760s,
they are of ancient man-
made origin with 18th-
century extensions and,
at farthest limits, a
Great Hall with alcove
statuary; see also in
vicinity **West Wycombe
House** (Sir Francis
Dashwood), Palladian
style with drifts of
spring flowers in
gardens (open June,
July, Aug.); **St**

Lawrence's church with
iron-age fort around it,
oriental temple interior,
good views from site;
and large but not too
inspiring **Dashwood
Mausoleum;** all the
above are on **West
Wycombe Nature Trail,**
4m (6.5km) long.

4m (6.5km) N on A4128

Hughenden Manor
Former home of
Benjamin Disraeli, who
is buried in churchyard
in park; house self-
consciously Gothic and
hardly to modern taste,
but pleasant walks along
terraces and through
woodland.

JUNCTION 5

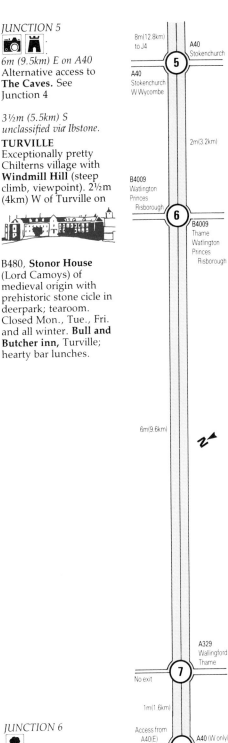

6m (9.5km) E on A40
Alternative access to
The Caves. See
Junction 4

*3½m (5.5km) S
unclassified via Ibstone.*
TURVILLE
Exceptionally pretty
Chilterns village with
Windmill Hill (steep
climb, viewpoint). 2½m
(4km) W of Turville on

B480, **Stonor House**
(Lord Camoys) of
medieval origin with
prehistoric stone cicle in
deerpark; tearoom.
Closed Mon., Tue., Fri.
and all winter. **Bull and
Butcher inn,** Turville;
hearty bar lunches.

*8m(12.8km)
to J4*

*A40
Stokenchurch*

5

*A40
Stokenchurch
W Wycombe*

2m(3.2km)

*B4009
Watlington
Princes
Risborough*

6

*B4009
Thame
Watlington
Princes
Risborough*

6m(9.6km)

*A329
Wallingford
Thame*

7

No exit

1m(1.6km)

*Access from
A40(E)*

A40 (W only)

wild flowers and
wildlife hereabouts;
woodland walks along
ancient **Ridge Way** on
NW escarpment of
Chilterns; dramatic
views; short distance S
(motorway underpass),
attractive picnic area in
**Cowleaze Wood;
Oxfordshire Way**
crosses Ridge Way and
follows old drove road
to Thames at
Henley-on-Thames.

JUNCTION 7

4m (6km) SW off A329

**Coach and Horses
motel,** Chislehampton.
16th-century inn is
nucleus of recent (1985)
motel development in
richly rural country;
genuinely 'county'
atmosphere; elaborate *à
la carte;* fairly expensive.
Tel: (0865) 890255.

*6m (9.6km) W and N off
A418*

**Waterperry Plant
Centre,** near Wheatley.
Former horticultural
school, now a short-
course centre for
gardening enthusiasts;
wide variety of conifers,
shrubs, roses, fruit
trees, soft fruits, herbs
and alpines; coffee, light
lunches, teas, highly
spoken of by food
writers; ornamental
gardens on River
Thame.

JUNCTION 6

2m (3km) E off A40
Beacon Hill Much
pleasant countryside,

M42:

Bromsgrove to Wilnecote, 31m (49.5km)

The M42 will one day be an important cross-country route from south-west to north-east England. At present it is little more than a partial ring road for the south and east of Birmingham, but work is in progress at both ends and further extensions will shortly be opened. The first part of the motorway, through a suburban landscape, gives access to the Shakespeare country. The second part, not so heavily trafficked, runs through tame agricultural country.

JUNCTION 1
6m (9.5km) NE on B4096 and A38
The Patrick Collection, King's Norton. See M5 Junction 4

JUNCTION 2
4m (7km) S off A441
National Needle Museum, Redditch. See M5 Junction 4

JUNCTION 3
6m (9.5km) S off A435
Alternative access to **National Needle Museum.** See M5 Junction 4

JUNCTION 4

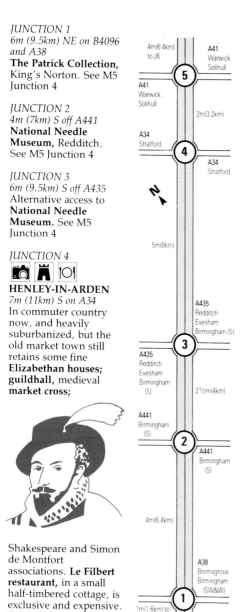

HENLEY-IN-ARDEN
7m (11km) S on A34
In commuter country now, and heavily suburbanized, but the old market town still retains some fine **Elizabethan houses; guildhall,** medieval **market cross;**

Shakespeare and Simon de Montfort associations. **Le Filbert restaurant,** in a small half-timbered cottage, is exclusive and expensive. Tel: (05642) 2700.

3m (5km) SE on B4439
Baddesley Clinton

Among the most admired of moated manor houses; much visited, entrance is often by numbered ticket. Closed Mon., Tue. and all winter.

JUNCTION 5

KNOWLE
2m (3km) S on A41
Knowle parish church Large and elaborate 14th-century chapel, exceptionally well-preserved; adjoined by equally interesting half-timbered **collegiate hall;** also worth looking at is Jacobean **Grimshaw Hall** (private), ½m (1km) W. Numerous 15th/16th-century architectural gems stand modestly in and around Knowle; **Chester House,** High Street, a fine early Tudor mansion, now a public library, is visitable. Closed Wed.

Map labels:
4m (6.4km) to J6
A41 Warwick Solihull
5
A41 Warwick Solihull
2m (3.2km)
A34 Stratford
4
A34 Stratford
5m (8km)
A435 Redditch Evesham Birmingham (S)
3
A435 Redditch Evesham Birmingham (S)
2½m (4km)
A441 Birmingham (S)
2
A441 Birmingham (S)
4m (6.4km)
A38 Bromsgrove Birmingham (SW&W)
1
1m (1.6km) to M5 (under construction)

JUNCTION 6

1m (1.5km) NW off A45

National Exhibition Centre, Birmingham. Modern equivalent of old British Industries Fair has permanent home in this impressive complex of exhibition halls; railway station, restaurants, hotels of startlingly up-to-date character; still developing.

3m (5km) E off A45
Meriden See M6 Junction 4

11m (17.5km) SE on A452

Kenilworth Castle
Famous and widespread shell of gigantic medieval citadel; *mise-en-scène* for events of Plantagenet, Barons' War, Wars of the Roses and Tudor times (see Scott's novel *Kenilworth)*; Strong Tower, White Hall, Mortimer's Tower and others are castles in themselves; half a day required to see the place properly.

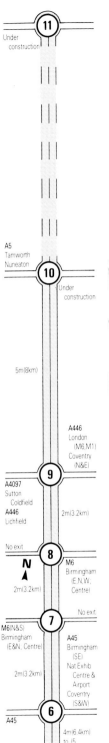

11 — Under construction

10 — A5 Tamworth Nuneaton — Under construction

5m(8km)

9 — A446 London (M6,M1) Coventry (N&E) — A4097 Sutton Coldfield — A446 Lichfield — 2m(3.2km)

8 — No exit — M6 Birmingham (E,N,W, Centre)

N

2m(3.2km) — No exit

7 — M6(N&S) Birmingham (E&N, Centre) — A45 Birmingham (SE) Nat Exhib Centre & Airport Coventry (S&W)

2m(3.2km)

6 — A45 — 4m(6.4km) to J5

JUNCTION 9
4m (6.5km) NE on A4097

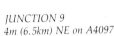

Kingsbury Water Park
Nature reserve and country park; visitor centre; aquatic activities; picnic area.

JUNCTION 10

2½m (4km) N across B5000 via Wilnecote

Alvecote Priory, near Tamworth. Dovecote and fragmentary ruin of priory on canal bank; chiefly worthwhile for the marked footpath among ponds and marshes, rich in botany and wildlife.

M45: Kilsby to Bourton-on-Dunsmore, 8m (13km)

In travelling days of old, Dunsmore was notorious for snowbound stage-coaches. Modern road engineering has changed all that and, compared with some of Britain's wild moorland, the heath country of Dunsmore is tame. Villages and meadowland of this corner of Warwickshire manage to preserve an air of serenity, though threatened by the offshoots of big manufacturing industries — automobile and electrical — of Rugby and Coventry.

When completed, the M45 will provide another link between London and the cities of the west Midlands and north-west England. At present it ends 10m (16km) short of Coventry.

JUNCTION 1

4m (6.5km) NE on A4071
Rugby School See M1 Junction 18

2m (3km) S off A45
Draycote Water Large and well-attended country park set up round biggest sheet of water in Warwickshire; sailing, fishing, nature trails; good views from hillside picnic areas.

4m (6.5km) SW on A423

Museum of Country Bygones, Marton. Old waggons, dairy equipment, collection of hand tools used in country crafts; thatching, shepherding, saddlery. Closed in winter.

7m (11km) SE on A45, recrossing motorway
Braunston A rejuvenated canal village near junction of Grand Union and Oxford canals; locks and tunnels; a favourite stopover for cruising boats.

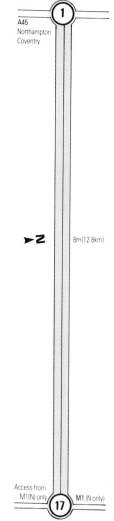

A45 Northampton Coventry

8m(12.8km)

Access from M1(N) only

M1 (N only)

13m (21km) W on A45, A445 and A444

Stoneleigh Abbey Contrast of monastic Tudor and neo-classical Georgian in this historic house (Lord Leigh); family in residence, but part open to visitors; gardens on Avon bank have ponds, maze, children's entertainments, walks; closed in winter.
National Agricultural Centre close by is home of Royal Agricultural Show (Aug.) and of **Farm and Country Centre** with livestock, botany, beekeeping, history, more serious and educational than most such centres.

2m (3km) E on A45
Dun Cow hotel, Dunchurch. Noted hostelry from way back; excellent bar lunch. Tel: (0788) 810203. Patrons look out on another house of low gables, formerly **Red Lion inn,** where Gunpowder Plot (1605) conspirators gathered and lay low until they learned of Guy Fawkes's capture.

M5:

Wednesbury to Exeter, 168m (269km)

To show a foreign visitor the essence of England in 3 hours, one could hardly do better than propose a run down the M5. It begins in the densely-populated Midlands, and then goes through, or close to, some of the most handsome and historic towns — Worcester, Cheltenham, Gloucester, Bristol, Taunton. It traverses a patriarchal countryside — the Malvern hills, the Vale of Severn, the Cotswolds and the Mendips. It touches at the holiday coasts of North Somerset and South Devon.

As the main route between the Midlands and the West Country, the M5 is at summer weekends barely adequate for the traffic it carries. Out of season, long stretches are relatively quiet; but the northern section, being also a great commercial highway, is usually fairly busy.

JUNCTION 1
BIRMINGHAM
4m (6.5km) E on A41
Access to city centre and, via inner ring road, to **Barber Institute of Fine Arts** and **Cadbury's chocolate factory.** See M6 Junction 6

JUNCTION 2

3m (5km) W on A459

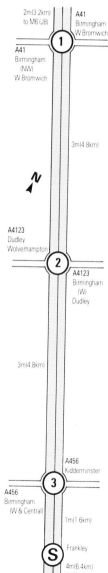

Dudley zoo and castle
Dudley pioneered zoo landscaping 50 years ago with 40 acres (16 hectares) of terraced rock and woodland round its 14th-century castle ruins; now a modest zoo by current standards, but still a pleasant, well-stocked layout; picnic areas; chairlift.

JUNCTION 3

6m (9.5km) W on A456, crossing many roundabouts

Hagley Hall Magnificent Georgian pile (Lord Cobham); portraits by old masters; exotic rococo decoration; finely-proportioned stable block where craftsmen (gunsmiths, clockmakers etc.) work in the old manner; temples, cascades in park; 'I cannot describe the enchanting beauties of Hagley Park,' wrote Horace Walpole; special events throughout summer include country fairs and vintage car rallies; pre-book lunch or dinner in house, minimum 8. Closed Sat. and all winter; open for pre-booked parties only in July and Aug. Tel: (0562) 882408

Road diagram labels:
2m(3.2km) to M6 (J8)
A41 Birmingham W Bromwich
(1)
A41 Birmingham (NW) W Bromwich
3m(4.8km)
A4123 Dudley Wolverhampton
(2)
A4123 Birmingham (W) Dudley
3m(4.8km)
A456 Kidderminster
(3)
A456 Birmingham (W & Central)
1m(1.6km)
(S) Frankley
4m(6.4km) to J4

M5: 4-5

5m (8km) E on A38 and B4121

4m(6.4km)
to services

A38
A491

4

A38
Birmingham
(S&SW)
Redditch &
M42
Bromsgrove
A491
Stourbridge

2½m(4km)

Under
construction

N

5m(8km)

3m (5km) NE on A38

The Patrick Collection,
Lifford Lane, King's
Norton. Select
exhibition of classic cars
old and new, including
rarities like the De
Lorean; poolside picnic
area; electronic games;
near junction of canals
and unusual guillotine
canal lock.

7m (11km) SE off A441

**National Needle
Museum,** Forge Mill,
Redditch. At the world
capital of needle
manufacture since dawn
of industry, the last
surviving needle mill
displays and operates
antiquated machinery;
site of 12th-century
Bordesley Abbey, being
excavated, is next door.

**Avoncroft Museum of
Buildings,** Stoke Heath.
'Heritage' array of full-
scale buildings of
various eras on a rural
site; medieval hall,
merchant's house,
cockpit, icehouse,
windmill, dovecote,
primitive privy,
horsedrawn caravans
and waggons, 1946 pre-
fab. Open Mar. to Nov.,
closed certain Mons. A
developing project.

2½m (4km) E on B4091

**Jinney Ring Craft
Centre,** Hanbury.
Farmstead sensitively
restored and reopened
as craft centre; glass,
pottery, wood,
paintings, knitwear;
coffee, tea, snack
lunches in kitchen.
Closed Mon. and Tue.
except during run-up to
Christmas.

2m (3km) SW on A38
Raven hotel and
restaurant, Droitwich.
Fine old black-and-white
building incorporating
historic manor-house; 55
well-appointed rooms;
recommended for
reasonably-priced
meals. Tel: (0905)
772224.

A38
Bromsgrove
Droitwich

5

A38
Droitwich

6m(9.6km)
to J6

JUNCTION 6

WORCESTER
4m (6.5km) W on A449 via Rainbow Hill

Busy cathedral city, parking difficult in tourist season; **cathedral** has spectacular Norman crypt, newly refurbished, also gift shop and tearoom; **river trips** from Diglis Basin, where Severn meets Worcester and Birmingham Canal; early Georgian **guildhall** and **assembly rooms;** **Tudor House Museum** of social history, closed Thur. and Sat.; **Commandery,** dignified Elizabethan hall on canal bank has audio-visuals, Civil War tableaux and in gardens a Civil War trail;

Worcester Royal Porcelain, Severn Street factory, guided tours and pottery exhibitions; good restaurant (tours and exhibitions summer only); **Brown's restaurant,** South Quay; in converted corn-mill; interesting atmosphere, good food if rather expensive. Tel: (0905) 26263.

6m(9.6km) to J5

A4538 Evesham A449 Worcester

6

A449 Kidderminster Worcester (N)

3m(4.8km)

2m (3km) SE on A422

Spetchley Park Graceful 18th-century house (private) in 30 acres (12 hectares) of rare foliage, best seen May/June; deer; teas on Suns.; closed in winter.

JUNCTION 7

3m (5km) NW on London Road, A44
Worcester See Junction 6

6m (9.6km) W on A44, signposted at Crown East Lane

Elgar's Birthplace, Lower Broadheath. Mss, scores, concert programmes, photographs, record shop. Closed Wed. and mid-Jan. to mid-Feb. Here begin **Elgar Route** (motoring) and **Elgar Trail** (walking), details at birthplace cottage.

10m (16km) SE on A44 and B4084
Blossom Route, Vale of Evesham. Circuit of 12m (19km) from Fladbury Cross (B4084) takes in Twyford, Harvington and other attractive villages, also punt ferry on Avon and striped maypole at Offenham; damson, plum and apple blossom is best Apr.-May.

A44 Worcester (S) Evesham

7

A44 Evesham Worcester (S)

8m(12.8km) to services

83

8m(12.8km)
to J7

(S) Strensham

1m(1.6km)

M50
S Wales
Ross

(8)

M50
S Wales
Ross

4m(6.4km)

N
▲

A438
Evesham
Tewkesbury

(9)

A438
Evesham
Tewkesbury

5m(8km)

No exit

(10)

A4019
Cheltenham

3m(4.8km)
to J11

JUNCTION 9

7m (11km) E off A435
'Ambridge' — proper name **Ashton under Hill.** Pretty village uncorrupted by renown as setting of never-ending radio serial *The*

Archers; towering yews and copper beeches; medieval church; high cross and antique sundial. Close by is Bredon Hill (1000ft (305m)) with **Parson's Folly,** a stone tower, on summit; easy climb to a view of A.E. Housman's 'coloured counties' (9 on a clear day).

1m (1½km) W on A438
Tewkesbury See M50 Junction 1

JUNCTION 10

1½m (2km) W on A4019

Coombe Hill Canal
Shortest canal in Britain, now a cutting rich in botany; site of special scientific interest.

3m (5km) W off A38
Deerhurst Quiet riverside village with largest surviving Saxon church; opposite, **Odda's Chapel** ruins (Odda, local Saxon earl, left inscription dating it to 1056).

CHELTENHAM
4m (6.5km) SE on A4019

Regency spa town, spaciously planned and extensively floral; **Montpellier Walk** has fine Regency shops divided by statuary; finery of beaux and belles at **Gallery of Fashion,** Pittville Pump Room; in Clarence

Road, **Gustav Holst Birthplace** furnished as composer knew it. **Eventos restaurant,** opposite town hall; plain fare well cooked, very reasonable prices. Tel: (0242) 570402.

7m (12km) S via Cheltenham at A435/A436 intersection
Seven Springs Stone-lined hollow with inscription; one of about 5 'authentic' sources of the Thames.

JUNCTION 11

3m (5km) E on A40
Cheltenham See
Junction 10

GLOUCESTER

3m (5km) W on A40
Superficially dull, with
cameos of venerable
history on closer
inspection; **New Inn
Lane** and **St Mary's
Gate,** with sagging
house-fronts; Beatrix
Potter's **Tailor of
Gloucester** house and
shop; **Folk Museum,**
Westgate Street; **New
Inn,** a medieval
'courtyard hostelry';
lovely stained glass in
cathedral's east

window; **Gloucester
Docks,** Britain's 'most
inland port'; **Century of**

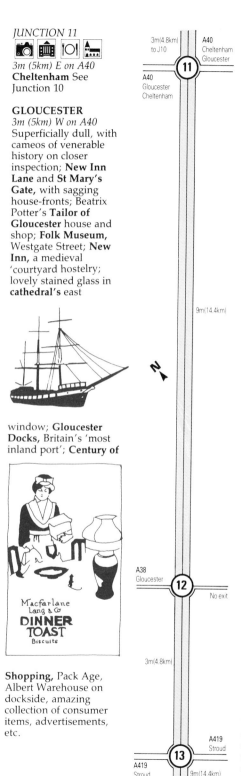

Macfarlane
Lang & Co
**DINNER
TOAST**
Biscuits

Shopping, Pack Age,
Albert Warehouse on
dockside, amazing
collection of consumer
items, advertisements,
etc.

3m(4.8km)
to J10

A40
Cheltenham
Gloucester

11

A40
Gloucester
Cheltenham

9m(14.4km)

A38
Gloucester

12

No exit

3m(4.8km)

A419
Stroud

13

A419
Stroud

9m(14.4km)
to services

JUNCTION 12

2m (3km) NW across A38
Stone Bench Viewpoint
for **Severn Bore;** waves
travel upriver at
irregular intervals,
depending on wind and
tidal conditions; a fairly
rare and unpredictable
phenomenon.

*5m (8km) NE crossing
motorway and via
Painswick, off A46*
Prinknash Abbey
Monastic settlement,
then private house (Earl
of Rothes), now an
abbey; good views NW
from monastery garden;
well-known commercial
pottery. **Country
Elephant restaurant,**
Painswick; superior
country cuisine, not too
expensive. Tel: (0452)
813564.

JUNCTION 13

2m (3km) W off A38
Frampton-on-Severn
Actually on Sharpness-
Gloucester ship canal;
attractive Vale of
Berkeley village on
Britain's largest village
green (22 acres (9
hectares)); **Frampton
Court,** handsome
Georgian house, adjoins
green; also **Manor Farm,**
birthplace of 'Fair
Rosamund', country girl
seduced by Henry II and
poisoned by his Queen
(1177).

5m (8km) W off A38

Wildfowl Trust,
Slimbridge. Best-known
of British wildfowl
reserves; viewing
towers; nature-related
activities; restaurant
where birds mingle with
customers.

JUNCTION 14

3m (5km) NW on B4509

Berkeley Castle
Ravaged 12th-century fortress-mansion, reeking of violent history; timbered great hall; terraced gardens; butterfly house, British and foreign species; unashamed tourist showplace, bit of a mêlée at times. Adjacent **church** has a detached tower and in village is unpretentious **Jenner Museum**, honouring locally-born vaccination pioneer. Castle closed Mon. and all winter.

3m (5km) SW on B4061
Thornbury Amid rash of housing estates, fine red sandstone **church** embosomed in noble

trees; **unfinished castle** — its owner, Duke of Buckingham, beheaded for treason during its construction. **Castle hotel** has good restaurant, prices not extortionate.

JUNCTION 16
6m (9.5km) S on A38
Bristol See M32 Junction 3

JUNCTION 17

6m (9.5km) S on A4018
Bristol Access to **Clifton**

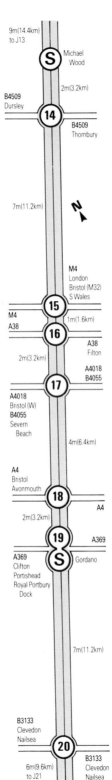

9m(14.4km) to J13

(S) Michael Wood

2m(3.2km)

B4509 Dursley

(14)

B4509 Thornbury

7m(11.2km)

N

M4 London Bristol (M32) S Wales

(15)

M4 A38

1m(1.6km)

(16)

A38 Filton

2m(3.2km)

A4018 B4055

(17)

A4018 Bristol (W) B4055 Severn Beach

4m(6.4km)

A4 Bristol Avonmouth

(18)

A4

2m(3.2km)

(19)

A369

A369 Clifton Portishead Royal Portbury Dock

(S) Gordano

7m(11.2km)

B3133 Clevedon Nailsea

(20)

B3133 Clevedon Nailsea

6m(9.6km) to J21

Down and **Clifton Zoo**. See M32 Junction 3

1½m (2.5km) S off A4018
Blaise Castle and Hamlet 18th/19th-century rural community neatly reconstructed; farmhouse, dairy etc.; educational.

JUNCTION 18

6m (9.5km) SE on A4
Bristol See M32 Junction 3. Road following Avon gorge with good access

to **Clifton Suspension Bridge**.

JUNCTION 19

7m (11km) E on A369
Bristol See M32 Junction 3. Road following south side of Avon gorge, with access to **Leigh Woods, Woodland trail** and **toll bridge** on Avon; also to ship *SS Great Britain*.

JUNCTION 20

CLEVEDON
½m (1km) W

Clevedon Court Parts of this manor house date from 12th century; gardens, rare shrubs; links with Tennyson and his *In Memoriam* friend Arthur Hallam; closed in winter. Close by in Moor Lane, **Clevedon Craft Centre** and **Yeo Pottery**; tearoom.

JUNCTION 21

WESTON-SUPER-MARE

5m (8km) W on A370
At N end of this holiday resort, on Kewstoke Road, **toll road** to woodland walks, seascapes, a pre-Roman camp; S end of town, 10th-century **Uphill Church,** closed in winter, good viewpoint; in Burlington Street, town centre,

Woodspring Museum has Punch and Judy, What the Butler Saw and similar amusing items from holidays of long ago.

JUNCTION 22

AXBRIDGE

8m (13km) NE on A38, recrossing motorway

Ancient houses; **Ambleside Water Gardens;** King John's Hunting Lodge has the local **museum. Oak House hotel,** opposite market hall; 12 small

quaint rooms; busy restaurant, first-class dishes from old-time country recipes. Tel: (0934) 732444.

10m (16km) E via Axbridge on A371
Cheddar Gorge Caves in deep limestone ravine, sadly commercialized but should be seen; **museum** with 10,000-year-old man; **adventure caving** offered; clifftop above **Jacob's Ladder** (274 steps) provides view of Mendips. E on A371 7m (11km) beyond Cheddar, **Wookey Hole,** spectacular caves, underground river (slightly awkward access); fairground, waxworks, Old Penny Pier Arcade, handmade paper-mill, café, souvenir shop.

JUNCTION 23

GLASTONBURY

15m (24km) E on A39

Township suffused in myth and legend; town centre **abbey** is oldest British sanctuary, supposed burial place of King Arthur; winter-flowering **thorn tree;**

rewarding climb to tower-crowned **Tor** (hill), 525ft (160m); **Somerset Rural Life Museum. No. 3 restaurant,** small but select, fairly costly *à la carte.* Tel: (0458) 32129.

M5: 24-25

JUNCTION 24

2m (3km) NW on A39
Bridgwater See
Junction 23

*6m (9.5km) SE on
unclassified road and A361*

'Alfred's Fort', Burrow
Bridge. Ruined church
of Isle of Athelney,
where Alfred
supposedly burned the
cakes; pumping station
nearby has small
museum with mid-19th-
century steam engines
which drained Somerset
Levels.

5m(8km)
to J23

(A39)
Minehead

(24)

A38
Bridgwater
Minehead

N

7m(11.2km)

A358
Taunton
Yeovil
Barnstaple
Honiton

(25)

A358
Taunton
Yeovil

5m(8km)
to services

Museum, North Street,
Taunton. History of
telephones from early
prototypes to latest
technology; Sat. only or
by appointment.

*8m (13km) E off A361
(signposted)*

Willow Craft Industry,
Mere Green Court, and
English Basket Centre,
Curload. Willows grown
and processed in
Somerset's oldest craft
industry; baskets and
artists' charcoal for sale.

*4m (6.5km) SW on minor
road, outskirts of Taunton*
Trull Quaint church,
curious Renaissance
carvings on bench-ends
and pulpit. 2m (3km) S
from Trull by footpath
or byroad (motorway
underpass),

Poundisford Park,
country house little
altered since 1546;
coach-house teas. Open
Wed., Thur., sometimes
Fri. but closed in winter.

*6m (9.5km) W on A358 via
Taunton*
West Somerset Railway,
Bishop's Lydeard. Old
GWR line through
Quantock hills to
Minehead, about 1½
hrs, lovingly restored
stock and stations; some
steam trains; daily
service in summer except
Sat., abbreviated
timetable at other times.

JUNCTION 25

2m (3km) W on A38

**Post Office
Telecommunications**

JUNCTION 26

1½m (2km) S on Blackdown hills

Wellington Monument
Steep climb to obelisk, 175ft (53m); viewfinder table aids identification of distant landmarks; Iron Duke took title from neighbouring town, with which he had no connection — they say its resemblance to his own name, Wellesley, attracted him.

6m (9.5km) SE on minor roads near Churchingford
Widcombe Tropical Bird Garden Parkland, ponds (flamingoes, swans); walled garden, restaurant, tea garden (parrots, cockatoos). Closed in winter.

2m (3km) N on A38

Sheppy's, Bradford-on-Tone. Cider farm, orchards, museum; shop sells cider, cheese and cream. Closed Sun. in winter.

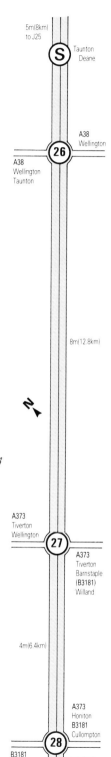

5m(8km) to J25

(S) Taunton Deane

A38 Wellington

(26)

A38 Wellington Taunton

8m(12.8km)

A373 Tiverton Wellington

(27)

A373 Tiverton Barnstaple (B3181) Willand

4m(6.4km)

A373 Honiton B3181 Cullompton

(28)

B3181 Cullompton

10m(16km) to J29

JUNCTION 27

TIVERTON
7m (11km) W on A373
Canal Country Park with horsedrawn trips in narrow boat from the Wharf, Canal Hill; **Tiverton Castle,** gaunt but inhabited (closed Fri., Sat., and winter); **Knightshayes Court,** Bolham, formal gardens, topiary work (closed Fri., and winter).

2m (3km) SE on B3391 at Uffculme
Coldharbour Mill
Historic establishment in rustic setting; exhibitions; waterside garden, cafeteria. Closed in winter, sometimes also Fri. and Sat.

JUNCTION 28

6m (9.5km) W on minor roads to A396
Bickleigh Castle Moated hall of Earls of Devon in picturesque Exe valley; now a museum of toys, model ships, agriculture, cloak-and-dagger gadgets, armour, old bicycles; in village,

Mill Craft Centre with fish farm and working oxen; cream teas. Castle closed Sat. and in winter; Craft Centre closed weekdays Christmas to Easter.

HONITON
11m (17.5km) E on A373
Georgian town of pottery and lace; 18th-century **pottery** and **Old Lace Shop** on main street; **Lace Museum,** All Hallows.

M5: *29-31*

JUNCTION 29

5m (8km) E off A30
Woodhayes restaurant,
Whimple. In small
hotel, varied menu, neat
presentation, average
prices. Tel: (0404)
822237.

JUNCTION 30

EXETER
*4m (6.5km) W on A30 and
B3183*

Rougemont House
reopens 1987 as
important museum of
costume and lace;
subterranean walks
under High Street along
route of city's medieval
water supply;

Maritime Museum,
Fishmarket (downhill from
cathedral) has real boats
of different lands, some
afloat; **Ship Inn,** Fore
Street (used by Sir
Francis Drake, serves
meals, tel: (0392) 55174)
and **St Nicholas Priory**
off Fore Street are good
examples of quaint old-
time Exeter.

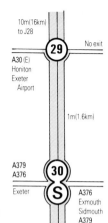

10m(16km)
to J28

29 No exit

A30 (E)
Honiton
Exeter
Airport

1m(1.6km)

A379
A376

30
S

Exeter
A376
Exmouth
Sidmouth
A379
Exeter
Dawlish

4m(6.4km)

N

A30
Okehampton
Barnstaple
(A377)
A38
Plymouth
Torquay
(A380)

31

7m (11km) S on A376

Country Life Museum,
Sandy Bay, Exmouth.
Rich assemblage of
historic vehicles,
implements; farm
animals; thatched
teashop; on seafront,

World of Miniature,
many little trains in
delightful artificial
landscapes. Closed in
winter.

JUNCTION 31

7m (11km) S on A379

Powderham Castle,
Kenton. Fortified house,
seat of Courtenays since
about 1400; coats of
arms, plasterwork, 18th-
century organ in chapel;
deer and wildfowl along
Kenn river and Exe
estuary; picnic areas.
Closed Fri., Sat. and all
winter.

M50:

**Strensham to Ross-on-Wye, 20m
(32km)**

This motorway has been described as Britain's most beautiful. It does appear an enticing prospect on the map, as it winds through the hop and cider country of Herefordshire and among quiet villages between Severn and Wye. But it runs mostly below the level of the surrounding landscape and is therefore most beautiful in the eyes of environmentalists — especially since from a short distance on either side one neither sees nor hears the traffic. The notable landmarks are the Malvern hills north of Junction 2. The central reservation becomes a corridor of wild daffodils in spring, and blossom from the orchards drifts across the carriageways.

JUNCTION 1

TEWKESBURY
3m (5km) S on A38
Archetypal English market town, retaining houses of some antiquity, mostly black-and-white; Mrs Craik's rags-to-riches novel *John Halifax, Gentleman* is still a good guide to the town, there portrayed as 'Nortonbury'; massive and austere **abbey church**, 12th-century; **Bloody Meadow** in loop of Avon where Battle of Tewkesbury (1471) ended Wars of the Roses.

UPTON-UPON-SEVERN
3m (5km) N on A38
Waterside township; river cruises and waterbus to Tewkesbury, Wed. through summer; many sailors at weekends; red

sandstone folly called **Pepperpot** at river bridge; Queen Anne **courthouse; Cromwell's** supply chocolates, handmade while you wait.

1½m(2.4km) to A5 (J8)

A38 Malvern

(1)

A38 Tewkesbury

N

9m(14.4km)

A417 Gloucester

(2)

A417 Ledbury Hereford (A438)

7½m(12km) to J3

JUNCTION 2

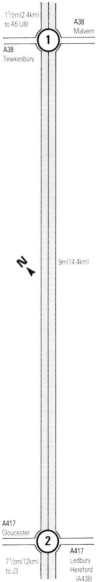

4m (6.5km) N off A417 and A438

Eastnor Castle Mock-medieval fortress under dramatic slope of Malvern hills; armour, carvings, tapestries; variegated woodland includes giant specimens. Open Sun. and bank holidays (also Wed. and Thur. in July and Aug.) or tel: Ledbury 2304 for appointment; closed in winter.

9m (14km) N via Ledbury and B4214

The Slatch, Bosbury. Old-world oasthouse and cottage with gardens, shrubs, pools and nine-acre **vineyard** producing white wine from Rhine, Moselle and French stock; visitors welcome, but should telephone first.

LEDBURY
4m (6.5km) N on A417

Somnolent old town with photogenic **market house; Knapp House,** birthplace of author John Masefield; medieval **Church Lane,** setting for some historical movies; **Collection Gallery,** 11 Southend, superior

art/craftwork; **Feathers hotel,** good value lunch in period ambience. Tel: (0531) 5266.

7m (11km) S off A417 at Hartpury

Ashleworth tithe barn Superb example of stone storehouses for ecclesiastical tithes; **church** and **courthouse** adjoining, the whole forming a unique group of Plantagenet-era monastic buildings.

7½m(12km) to J2

B4221 Newent

③

B4221 Newent

2 ◀

3½m(5.6km)

A449 S Wales Ross Monmouth

④

JUNCTION 3

KEMPLEY
2m (3km) N unclassified
Tiny Norman **church** of St Mary the Virgin with recently-uncovered 12th-century frescoes, 1m (1.5km) N of present village; curious 'scob' (oak-trunk parish strongbox) in vestry; another 1m (1.5km) N, at Much Marcle, **hollow yew** seating 7.

3m (5km) SE near Newent on B4216
Falconry Centre Birds of prey, aviaries, museum, picnic area. Closed Tue. and all winter. At 31 Culver Street, Newent, **Cowdy Shop,** famed for delicate glassware.

JUNCTION 4

ROSS-ON-WYE
½m (1km) SW
At this busy market and tourist centre, the A40 **Wye Valley Route** to Monmouth and Chepstow begins (for southern section, A466, see M4 Junction 22); at 3m (5km), tottering wreck of **Goodrich Castle,** fortress of Welsh

Marches; 1½m (2.5km) on, **Symonds Yat** (it probably means 'gate'), horseshoe bend of Wye in wooded valley; close by, **Jubilee Maze** of pathways to central temple, opened 1981; and **World of Butterflies** in covered garden.

M53:

Wallasey to Chester, 20m (32km)

Liverpool Bay, the Mersey estuary and the Sands of Dee are all within hailing distance, but this motorway sees little of the sea as it courses through the Wirral peninsula. It begins near the seaside resorts of New Brighton and Hoylake.

The route is thickly populated and industrialized. Most of its junctions are crowded together in the region of Ellesmere Port and Eastham, where the Manchester Ship Canal reaches the sea. Towards the end of the route (Junctions 10 to 12) there are glimpses of pastoral Cheshire and a dramatic view of the walls round Chester, a great tourist city.

JUNCTION 1

10m (16km) W to West Kirby on A540
Hilbre Island Actually 3 islands, postage-stamp size; access on foot at low tide (best from Dee Lane slipway, West Kirby, where tide-tables are posted); must have prior permission (written requests only) from Tourist Office, P.O. Box 100, Wirral; islands are a fascinating nature reserve and haunt of wading birds; round trip on foot, from West Kirby and back, 5m (8km).

JUNCTION 2

8m (13km) W on B5139
Alternative route to **Hilbre Island.** See Junction 1

5m (8km) W on A540
Red Rocks, Hoylake. One of the best beaches in the north-west.

JUNCTION 3

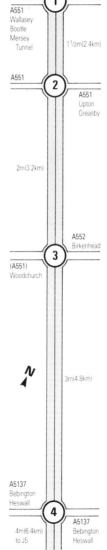

2½m (4km) E on A552
Birkenhead Park, Park Road, N end of town. An unusually large park and unconventional in design (by Paxton). **Lincluden guesthouse,** Storeton Road, Prenton, Birkenhead is a convenient establishment; 17 rooms; reasonable charges. Tel: (051) 608 3732.

JUNCTION 4

PORT SUNLIGHT
2½m (4km) E on A5137 and A41

Model village created by Lord Leverhulme (Sunlight Soap); history unfolds in Edwardian-Tudor **Heritage Centre**

and Pantheon-like **Lady Lever Art Gallery** (Chinese and Wedgwood pottery, 18th-century furniture).

1m (1.5km) W on A5137
Brimstage Hall Noted for 14th-century rectangular tower; guided tours, Wed. only; inside, open Tue.-Fri. inclusive. The 'Country Mouse' embroidery centre, needlework demonstrated, coffee shop and gift shop.

M53: 5-10

JUNCTION 5

PARKGATE
6m (9.5km) W on B5133
Village on Dee Sands,
once a major port for
Ireland; sea has receded
but visitors still come;
noted for shrimp teas
and ice-cream — and for
being different from
Hoylake and New
Brighton. **Boat House
restaurant,** The Parade,
offers seascapes and a
Continental cuisine. Tel:
(051) 336 3814.

5m (8km) W on B5133

Ness Gardens, Neston.
Liverpool University
botanic garden; visitor
centre; slide show;
magnolias, camellias,
large heather garden;
hothouses opened on
request; refreshments in
summer.

JUNCTION 6

6m (10km) W on B5133
Ness Gardens, Neston.
See Junction 5. Neston
is also on **Wirral
Country Park** route
(12m (19km)), a linear
park with footpath
above shore; wide views

over Dee estuary; starts
at Hooton station on
B5133 and ends at West
Kirby.

JUNCTIONS 7, 8 and 9
Three contiguous
junctions serving
Ellesmere Port. Best exit
is 9.

JUNCTION 9

ELLESMERE PORT
½m (1km) E on A5032

Boat Museum on old
Shropshire Union Canal
basin near entrance to
Manchester Ship Canal
— historic interchange
of waterways
connecting with
London, Midlands and
the North; about 50 old
barges tied up, open to
inspection; exhibition
covers water transport
generally.

JUNCTION 10

*4m (6.5km) W on A5117
and S to entrance on A41,
signposted*

Chester Zoo One of the
oldest; spectacular floral
displays; waterbus
penetrates habitats of
wildfowl; **Oakfield** a
good restaurant as Zoo
restaurants go; snack
bars, picnic lawns.

Map (centre column)

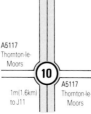

4m(6.4km) to J4

A41 Bebington Chester (A550)

5

A41 Chester Bebington (A550)

1m(1.6km)

Local roads — Local roads

6

2m(3.2km)

B5132 Overpool

7

B5132 Overpool

1m(1.6km)

A5032 Little Sutton

8

A5032 Little Sutton

1m(1.6km)

A5032 Ellesmere Port

9

A5032 Ellesmere Port

3m(4.8km)

A5117 Thornton-le-Moors

10

A5117 Thornton-le-Moors

1m(1.6km) to J11

JUNCTION 12

CHESTER
2m (3km) W on A56

Enthralling walled city full of intricate alleyways and shops of country character; carparks inside the **walls,** which may be walked; **rows** in Watergate, Bridge and Eastgate Streets, 2-tiered shops, upper tiers set back to allow balcony promenade and view of city-centre bustle; **visitor centre,** Vicars Lane, for audio-visual city history, with restaurant; history very much alive in streets — **Town Crier** performs twice a day, 'Roman' soldiers patrol the walls, volunteer guides at visitor centre offer guided walks; scores of antiquated buildings and tottering inns;

cathedral, purplish walls, amusingly-carved choirstalls, was a church in Saxon times; **Grosvenor Park,** off Vicars Lane on Deeside, three times winner of 'Britain in Bloom'

1m(1.6km) to J10

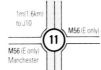
11
M56 (E only)

M56 (E only) Manchester

M56 (E only)

3m(4.8km)

A56 Helsby Chester (A41) (A55)

12

contest; at **Tower Wharf,** N of Watergate,

horse-drawn barges through ancient heart of city; **pleasure cruises** on Dee from landing stages near Grosvenor Park and Queen's Park bridge; many restaurants, tearooms, cafés and home bakeries, among them **Witches Kitchen,** Frodsham Street, end of Eastgate, for all-day bistro cuisine swiftly and cheerfully served.

M54:

Essington to Wellington, 23m (37km)

From the fringe towns of the Black Country (which is no longer very black) and the M6 north of Birmingham, this motorway follows the route of the ancient London-Chester-Holyhead highway and the even more ancient Watling Street (A5) as far as the green countryside of Shropshire. Here, however, industry appears again in the shape of old coalfields and iron workings which have been gathered together in the 'new town' of Telford. Peaceful scenes are always within reach. Decayed villages and country houses hold memories of King Charles II's wanderings after the Battle of Worcester (1651), as several 'Royal Oak' inn-signs testify. The M54 has 8 junctions, no fewer than 4 of them serving Telford New Town.

JUNCTION 1

10m (16km) NE on A460 and A5
Chasewater Leisure Park See M6 Junction 11

JUNCTION 2
7m (11km) N on A449 to Penkridge and NE unclassified to Brocton
Access to most picturesque parts of **Cannock Chase.** See M6 Junction 11

1½m (2.5km) SE off A449

Moseley Old Hall
Typical Midlands manor-house of Tudor period; ornamental water; Charles II hid here after Worcester. Open Wed., Thur., Sat. in summer, Sun. only in winter.

JUNCTION 3

¼m (½km) N on A41

A41
Whitchurch
Weston

③

5m(8km)
to J4

A41
Wolverhampton
(W)

➤Z

8m(12.8km)

A449
M6 (North)
Wolverhampton
Stafford

②

A449
Wolverhampton

1½m(2.4km)

A460
Cannock

①

A460
Cannock

2m(3.2km)
to M6 (J10A)

Tong Many knightly tombs in **church,** which is scarred with Civil War cannonshot; Dickens's *Old Curiosity Shop* ended here and churchyard is fictional resting place of Little Nell.

1½m (2.5km) S off A41
Aerospace Museum, Cosford. Large collection of aircraft and equipment at former RAF station; rare prototypes; missiles; shop sells model kits; café. Open daily in summer, closed weekends in winter.

3m (5km) N to A41 and E from Tong Norton

Boscobel House Modest 17th-century gentleman's residence where Charles II took refuge; offshoot of 'Royal Oak' in park; close at hand, **White Ladies,** historic nunnery; also **Chillington Castle,** Georgian, with lake and great oaks in park; home of celebrated Chillington herd of wild white cattle, now almost extinct. Open Thur., occasionally Sun., summer only.

JUNCTION 4

IRONBRIDGE
6m (9.5km) S on A464 and A442

Cradle of Industrial Revolution, thanks to discovery of iron-smelting techniques in **Coalbrookdale** in 1709;

on Severn gorge, the world's first **cast-iron bridge,** considered a miracle when built (1779); complex of prize-winning museums round about commemorates first iron steam engine, boat and railway wheels; **Coalport China Tar Tunnel** 2m (3km) away (it was cut for water, but bitumen came out); **Blists Hill** village (1½m (2.5km)) clanks with reconstructed machinery; altogether a strange little world of industrial archaeology, worthy winner of a European Museum of the Year award.

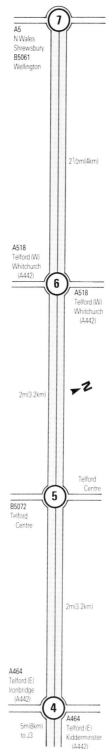

A5
N Wales
Shrewsbury
B5061
Wellington

2½m(4km)

A518
Telford (W)
Whitchurch
(A442)

A518
Telford (W)
Whitchurch
(A442)

2m(3.2km)

Telford
Centre

B5072
Telford
Centre

2m(3.2km)

A464
Telford (E)
Ironbridge
(A442)

5m(8km)
to J3

A464
Telford (E)
Kidderminster
(A442)

12m (19km) S on A442

Severn Valley Railway, Bridgnorth. Restored steam line, regular timetable, 20 trains a day in summer; restaurant car on Sun., Mar.-Oct.; delightful trip of 16m (29km) through Severn Vale, touching at 1 elegant town (Bewdley) and 2 outstandingly pretty villages (Arley and Hampton Loade).

JUNCTION 6
5m (8km) via Telford (recrossing motorway) on A4169
Alternative access to **Ironbridge.** See Junction 4

JUNCTION 7

5m (8km) W on A5 and B4380
Wroxeter Extensive excavations and reconstructions, still proceeding, of fourth largest city of Roman Britain; legionary stronghold; uniquely, in a totally rural setting.

6m (9.5km) S to B4380 via unclassified pleasant lanes Under forest fleece of **Wrekin** (1334ft (407m)), an isolated ridge.

Buildwas Abbey graceful Norman ruin in serene environment on Severn bank. Access via Buildwas to **Ironbridge,** a further 3m (5km). See Junction 4

M55:

Fulwood to Blackpool, 13m (21km)

The landscape of the route seems to belong more to the other side of England — the Lincolnshire or East Anglian fenlands, merging with a shallow sea. Long ago it was a great marshland whose waters seeped out to, or more often in from, the Wyre (river of Fleetwood) to the north and the Ribble (river of Preston) to the south.

The M55 countryside, called Fylde (field), is dotted with smallholdings, poultry-houses and hamlets; a land where people have done nothing much but mind their own business since time began. Little to be expected, therefore, of historic or scenic attractions. In summer holidaymakers thunder down to Blackpool, Lytham St Anne's and Thornton Cleveleys.

The M55 has 4 junctions, counting the 2 at each end. It leaves the M6 at a point notorious for traffic queues at holiday times and it ends within a short distance of Blackpool's 'Golden Mile'. The 2 intermediate junctions are currently labelled 1, and 3.

JUNCTION 1

|O| |🌳|

1m (1.5km) N on A6
The Orchard restaurant, Whittingham Lane, Broughton. Conventional fare conscientiously prepared and served at small haven of quietness between busy motorways; moderate charges.

11m (17.5km) N on A6 to Broughton, E (crossing M6) through network of lanes, signposted

Beacon Fell Country Park A breath of Bowland Forest air; conifers, open moorland; walks round and to the Fell (873ft, 266m); ranger on duty; information centre; refreshments Sun. and most summer weekdays.

4m (7km) S on A6
Preston See M6 Junction 31

1m(1.6km) to M6 (J32)

A6 Preston Garstang

(1)

A6 Preston Garstang

N◄

7m(11.2km)

A585 Kirkham

(3)

4m(6.4km) to J4

A585 Kirkham Fleetwood

JUNCTION 3

|📷| |🏛| |O|

FLEETWOOD
14m (22.5km) N on A585 and A588
Traditional market held Mon., Sat. in summer, Tue., Fri. all year; acres of stalls and bargains.

Museum, Dock Street; 150-year history of this important fishing port.

6m (10km) S via Kirkham, off A585
Ledra restaurant, Freckleton. Not cheap, but has long maintained a reputation for high-class cuisine.

4m(6.4km)
to J3

JUNCTION 4

(Blackpool terminus)
LYTHAM ST ANNE'S
5m (8km) S on A583

Ashton Gardens, near
pier; small area of
rockeries, roses and
waterplants. **Nature
reserve,** off Clifton
Drive North; maritime
flora and fauna. Historic

Windmill, Lytham
Green, serves as
information centre and
museum and is working
again.

BLACKPOOL
4m (6.5km) W on A583

Many things to many
people — noisy, vulgar,
affirmation of innate
optimism of human
race; slot-machine
capital of Europe. Amid
froth and glitter it is
worth seeking out
Stanley Park, 1m
(1.5km) from motorway
off West Park Drive; 250
acres (101 hectares) of
expensively-laid-out
public gardens with
lake, statuary and
renowned Italian and
Rose Gardens; also

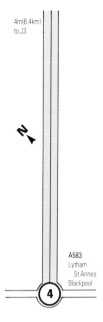

A583
Lytham
St Annes
Blackpool

open-plan Zoo, which
has Europe's most
modern layout; **Grundy
Art Gallery,** Queen
Street, rare netsuki and
ivories, never
mentioned in brochures;
and the Blackpool

trams, vintage and ultra-
modern, various shapes
and sizes, travelling
seafront roads
northward to Fleetwood
(12m (19km)).

M56:
Cheadle to Capenhurst, 35m (54km)

This important and busy route links the southern towns of the Manchester conurbation with the estuary of the Dee, west of Chester, just short of Wales. In summer it carries many thousands of Lancastrians to and from their traditional North Welsh holiday resorts. Although the route passes over the northern Cheshire plain and close to the rolling country of Delamere Forest, it is either urban or suburban for nearly the whole way. Only in the neighbourhood of Chester (Junctions 14 and 15) do built-up areas begin to thin out. Junctions are numbered 1 to 16, except for 13 which is presently missing. Access to and exit from the first 4 are severely limited and Junction 5 serves only Manchester airport.

JUNCTION 1
7m (11km) N on A34
Manchester Access to city centre and east side. See M602, terminal junction.

JUNCTION 2

2m (3km) N on A5103
Fletcher Moss Art Gallery, Didsbury. Housed in a neat old parsonage; maps and prints of historic Manchester; Lowry paintings; pottery and glass of locality, various periods; botanical garden with orchids round the house. Closed in winter.

1m (1.5km) W on A560

Wythenshawe Horticultural Centre, Altrincham Road. Not a commercial garden centre but run by Manchester Corporation; glasshouses contain pineapples, bananas, coffee beans and other exotica; cactus house has the Charles Darrah Bequest.

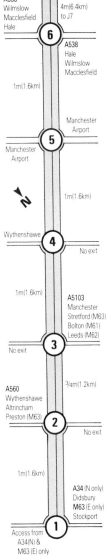

A538
Wilmslow
Macclesfield
Hale

(6)

4m(6.4km)
to J7

A538
Hale
Wilmslow
Macclesfield

1m(1.6km)

(5)

Manchester
Airport

Manchester
Airport

N

1m(1.6km)

Wythenshawe

(4)

No exit

1m(1.6km)

A5103
Manchester
Stretford (M63)
Bolton (M61)
Leeds (M62)

(3)

No exit

3/4m(1.2km)

A560
Wythenshawe
Altrincham
Preston (M63)

(2)

No exit

1m(1.6km)

A34 (N only)
Didsbury
M63 (E only)
Stockport

(1)

Access from
A34(N) &
M63 (E) only

JUNCTION 3

2m (3km) N on A5103
Fletcher Moss Art Gallery See Junction 2

1m (1.5km) W on A560
Wythenshawe Horticultural Centre See Junction 2

7m (11km) N on A5103
Manchester Access to centre and west side. **Castlefield** (arts/leisure/museum complex) is best approached from this junction. See M602, terminal junction.

JUNCTION 4
½m (1km) W (unclassified)
Wythenshawe Horticultural Centre Alternative access. See Junction 2

JUNCTION 5
Manchester Airport

JUNCTION 6

7m (11km) SE on A538 and B5166
Styal Country Park A patch of unspoiled countryside within Greater Manchester; incorporates **Quarry Bank Mill**, restored with looms at full blast and all the dust and clatter of the cotton-spinning heyday. Closed Mon. except in high summer.

JUNCTION 7

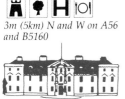

3m (5km) N and W on A56 and B5160

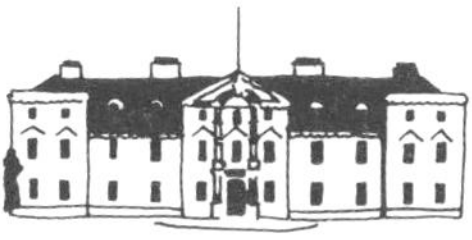

Dunham Massey Hall, near Altrincham. Late Earl of Stamford, now National Trust property, well signposted; elegant Queen Anne mansion; valuable Huguenot silver; kitchen and corn mill refurbished; gardens, park; restaurant in stables; one of the great estates. Closed in winter. **Beech Mount hotel,** Barrington Road, Altrincham. Airport executives like to eat there and they usually know what's what; rather expensive. Tel: (061) 928 4523.

3m (5km) S on A556 and A6034
Tatton Park See M6 Junction 19

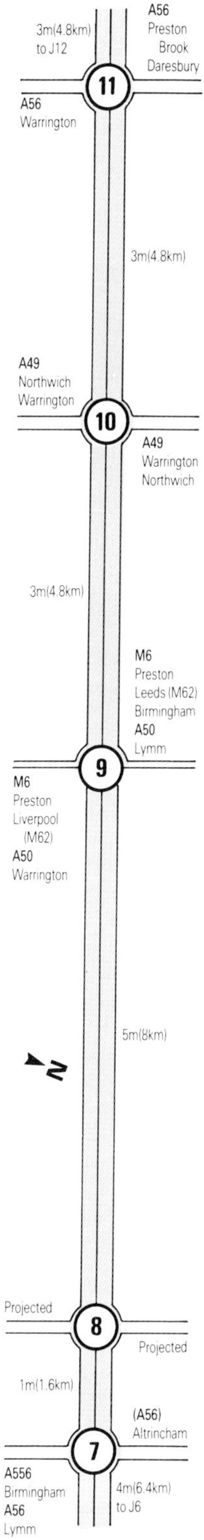
3m(4.8km) to J12
A56
Preston
Brook
Daresbury
11
A56
Warrington
3m(4.8km)
A49
Northwich
Warrington
10
A49
Warrington
Northwich
3m(4.8km)
M6
Preston
Leeds (M62)
Birmingham
A50
Lymm
9
M6
Preston
Liverpool
(M62)
A50
Warrington
5m(8km)
N
Projected
8
Projected
1m(1.6km)
(A56)
Altrincham
7
A556
Birmingham
A56
Lymm
4m(6.4km)
to J6

JUNCTION 10

9m (14.5km) SE on A559, outskirts of Northwich
Anderton Lift
Extraordinary piece of civil engineering; lifts barges bodily between 2 canals; not often working, unfortunately.

8m (13km) S on A559 and E at Four Lanes

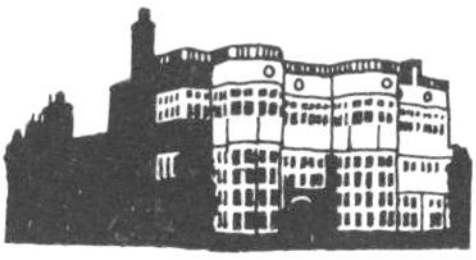

Arley Hall and Gardens
Stately Victorian-Tudor hall, private chapel and real Tudor barn; beautiful park, magnificent gardens; blacksmith and carpenter at work; teas in barn. Closed Mon. and all winter.

JUNCTION 11

DARESBURY
1m (1.5km) N on A56
Village birthplace of Lewis Carroll — he would hardly recognize the place now; **All Saints Church** has 16th-century tower and, more notably, a richly-coloured and whimsical stained-glass window

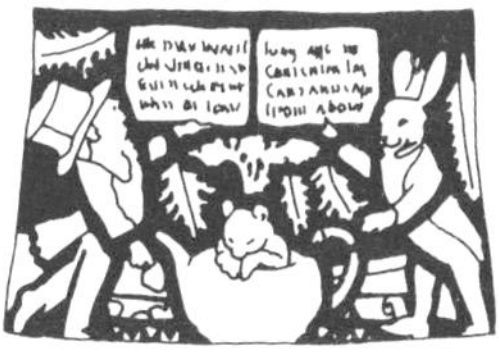

with *Alice in Wonderland* scenes.

¼m (0.5km) S on A58
Preston on the Hill
Canalside village and boat-hire centre on popular Trent and Mersey canal.

M56: *12-16*

FRODSHAM

1½m (2.5km) S on A56
New and enterprising
arts centre in **Castle
Park Gardens,** formerly
grounds of a country
house. **Frodsham Hill**
offers sandstone rock-
climbing to both novices

and experts. **Old Hall
Hotel** in tree-lined main
street; ancient building
successfully
modernized; 20 rooms;
real value for money for
lunch or dinner. Tel:
(0928) 32052.

*2m (3km) N on A557 (at
Runcorn, follow signposts
E)*

Norton Priory Stylish
museum, opened 1982,
on monastic site; fine
Norman doorway
among excavated
masonry; statuary, bell
and other medieval-
religious souvenirs;
woodland garden with
footpath to historic
Bridgewater Canal; a
small museum
award-winner.

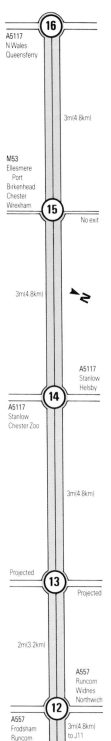

16

A5117
N Wales
Queensferry

3m(4.8km)

M53
Ellesmere
Port
Birkenhead
Chester
Wrexham

15

No exit

3m(4.8km)

N

A5117
Stanlow
Helsby

14

A5117
Stanlow
Chester Zoo

3m(4.8km)

Projected

13

Projected

2m(3.2km)

A557
Runcorn
Widnes
Northwich

12

A557
Frodsham
Runcorn
Widnes

3m(4.8km)
to J11

2m (3km) E off A56
Helsby Hill Wooded
ridge (460ft (140m)),
easy to climb; splendid
views over Merseyside
and Vale Royal of
Cheshire; **iron-age fort**
on summit; from this
hill the 32m (51km)
Sandstone Trail goes S
through Delamere
Forest to Shropshire
border.

*4½m (7km) S and E on
A56 and minor roads to
Mouldsworth*

**Mouldsworth Motor
Museum** Small but
select old motor and
motor-cycle collection;
bric-à-brac of motoring
nostalgia; open p.m.
Sun. only.

*4m (6.5km) S on A540 and
E following signs*
Chester Zoo See M53
Junction 10

HAWARDEN

*7m (11km) SW and E on
A5117 and A550*
Ruins of **Hawarden
Castle,** fortress of the
Welsh Marches. Village
has links with W.E.
Gladstone, Victorian
prime minister, who
lived at the **Hall.**

M57:
Huyton to Aintree, 9m (14.5km)

This motorway travels across the outskirts of Liverpool, linking the 2 east-going Lancashire motorways M62 and M58. The route is not entirely built-up; there are still a few green spaces in the outer suburbs of Liverpool. The area was favoured by the shipowners and merchants of long ago, so it may be said that some country houses were built on coffin ships and the slave trade. But housing developments and light-industrial zones have encroached on the old estates. Junctions on the M57 have no numbers; we have numbered them in brackets, for convenience. There are exit and access points in 6 places, including the 2 meeting-points with M62 and M58.

JUNCTION (2)

½m (1km) E on A57

Prescot Museum of Clock and Watchmaking, 34 Church Street, Prescot. A new museum with study and library facilities; chiefly for the enthusiast, but the worker's life in a bygone era is evoked and his tools and equipment are displayed. Closed Mon.

1m (1.5km) E on A58 (Prescot bypass)
Knowsley Safari Park Animal-lovers will be content with driving through the large park, where the customary safari-park denizens roam; special emphasis on eland and wildebeeste; parking and spacious picnic area outside game reserves; fairground, domestic animals; dolphin shows most days; cafeteria. Closed Nov.-Feb.

No exit

3m(4.8km) to J4

③ *B5198 (A57) Knotty Ash*

1½m(2.4km)

A57 Knotty Ash (A58) St Helens (B5199) Huyton

② *A57*

2m(3.2km) to J1 M62(J6)

5m (8km) E on A58

Pilkington Glass Museum, Prescot Road, St Helens. A big name in glass worldwide, at hub of Britain's glass and chemicals industries; a serious industrial museum with beautiful examples of important works in glass; exhibitions show old and new in hand-pressing and press-moulding techniques, iridescent 'carnival' glass; also 'Rocking Horses through the Ages', picture embroidery; gift shop, glass souvenirs. Closed Christmas to New Year.

8m (13km) W on A57
Liverpool Access via Knotty Ash, see M62 Junction 4. Turn S on Liverpool Ring Road for **Albert Dock Village** and **Merseyside Maritime Museum** (see M62 Junction 4) and for **Transworld Festival Gardens** and **Speke Hall** (see M62 Junction 5).

M57: (4)-(6)

JUNCTION (4)

8m (13km) E on A580 and A570 to St Helens
Pilkington Glass Museum See Junction (2)

6m (9.5km) W on A580
Liverpool Access to city centre via Walton. See M62 Junction 4

2½m (4km) W on A580 and Lower House Lane, signposted

Croxteth Hall and Country Park Large dignified Hall (former Earls of Sefton) with Edwardian facade; Croxteth Heritage exhibition and audio-visual show presents old-time life above and below stairs; sporting memorabilia; crafts and carriages in courtyard; award-winning walled garden (espaliers, figs, peaches, mushroom house); Home Farm with docile livestock; guided walks through park (rhododendrons in May and June); riding instruction; amusing train rides in scaled-down 'Little Train' of Wales; picnic area. Closed in winter, except for Heritage and Home Farm.

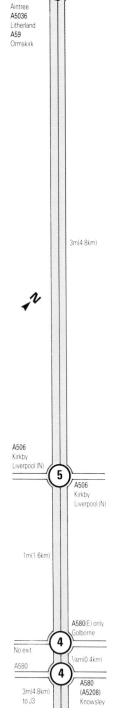

A59
Aintree
A5036
Litherland
A59
Ormskirk

3m(4.8km)

A506
Kirkby
Liverpool (N)

A506
Kirkby
Liverpool (N)

1m(1.6km)

A580(E) only
Golborne

No exit

A580

¼m(0.4km)

A580
(A5208)
Knowsley

3m(4.8km)
to J3

JUNCTION (5)
5m (8km) W on A506
Liverpool Access to north of city. See M62 Junction 4

JUNCTION (6)

10m (16km) W on A5036 and N to coast
Waterloo and **Crosby.** These residential suburbs of Liverpool have broad expanses of

sand stretching uninterrupted for several miles northward.

6m (9.5km) N on A59

Aughton Park Contains well-known garden called Cranford; unique layout; a riot of roses and flowering shrubs in season. Closed in winter.

M58:

Aintree to Wigan, 12½m (19km)

This is the fourth side of the Merseyside quadrilateral of motorways, the other sides being made up of the M57, M62 and M6. It begins on the northern edge of Liverpool and traverses agricultural country before entering the industrial belt near Skelmersdale. The unnumbered western terminus coincides with the last junction on the M57 (also unnumbered). The 4 intermediate junctions are numbered 1, 3, 4 and 5; and the route ends at the M6 on the outskirts of Wigan. All Lancashire motorways are busy, but the M58 is less busy than most.

JUNCTION 1
5m (8km) N on B5197
Alternative access to
Aughton Park. See M57
Junction (6)

JUNCTION 3
8m (13km) S on A570
Pilkington Glass Museum, St Helens.
See M57 Junction (2)

11m (17.5km) N on B5240 and A59
Rufford Old Hall See
M6 Junction 27

9m (14.5km) N on B5240 and A59 (signposted at Burscough Bridge)
Martin Mere (Wildfowl Trust). See M6
Junction 27

JUNCTION 6
3m (5km) E on A577 and A49
Wigan Pier See M6
Junction 25

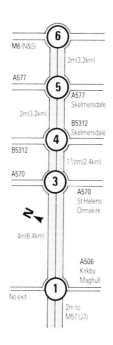

A57(M):

Manchester, 1½m (2.5km)

Motorway status is accorded to this urban through-route, the Mancunian Way, south of Manchester city centre. Its western terminus is on the Chester Road, very close to the Urban Heritage Park at Castlefield (see M602, terminal junction). Its eastern terminus leads to the Ashton-under-Lyne highway, A635 (see Ashton-under-Lyne on M67 Junction 1).

The Mancunian Way's 3 intermediate junctions, unnumbered, give access to the M63 Junction 9, the M56 Junction 1 and the M63 Junction 12.

A58(M):

Leeds inner ring road (west), ½m (.75km)

A64(M):

Leeds inner ring road (east), ½m (.75km)

Britain's shortest motorway routes are joined together to provide a semicircular detour round the heart of Leeds, carrying east-west traffic just north of the city centre. More than half of the A58(M) is in a tunnel. You would not normally make for these motorways in order to gain access to 'best off' places of interest, but the following worthwhile sites are conveniently reached from each end.

A58(M) terminus (west)
½m (1km) W on A65
Kirkstall Road
Armley Mills See M621
Junction 2

1m (1.5km) W on A65
Kirkstall Road
Kirkstall Abbey and
Abbey House See M621
Junction 2

A64(M) terminus (east)
4m (7km) E on A64 York
Road and A63
Temple Newsam See
M62 Junction 30

3m (5km) N on A58
Roundhay Road

Roundhay Park
Extensive parkland with lake, canal gardens, roses, fishponds, tropical house; a public park renowned far beyond the limits of Leeds; many and varied summer events.

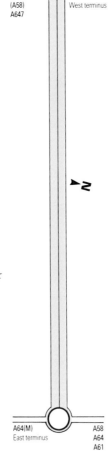

A62	A58(M)
(A58)	West terminus
A647	

A64(M)	A58
East terminus	A64
	A61

7m (11km) N on A61,
following signposts for
Harrogate

Harewood House One of England's best-known and most-visited Palladian mansions (Earl of Harewood); bird garden with a host of species from owls to penguins; paradise garden of reptiles and small mammals; house open only in summer.

3m (5km) E on A64 York
Road and A63
Rules restaurant, Selby Road; civilized, Continental flavour, medium-priced. Tel: (0532) 604564

M6: Lilbourne to Carlisle, 238m (373km), including A38(M) (Birmingham), 2m (3km).

The M6 branches off from the M1 at Junction 19, east of Rugby. A short stretch of pretty Warwickshire countryside is followed by the sprawling cities of Coventry and Birmingham and then the Black Country — almost 30m (48km) of towns and traffic, slow-moving around 9 am and 5 pm. Rural parts of Staffordshire are attractive. The M6 travels round the Potteries and close to the manufacturing towns of Lancashire. Traffic density high on these sections.

North of Lancaster the route acquires a breezy moorland character as it skirts the Lake District. Near Shap Fell (1827ft (590m)) the hilly topography separates northbound and southbound carriageways from each other for several miles. Little is seen of Carlisle and the M6 ends just short of Gretna Green on the Scottish border. The section between Junctions 30 and 32 (Preston bypass) was the first motorway built in Britain.

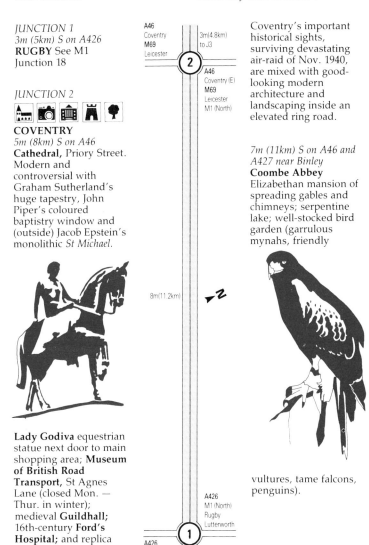

JUNCTION 1
3m (5km) S on A426
RUGBY See M1
Junction 18

JUNCTION 2

COVENTRY
5m (8km) S on A46
Cathedral, Priory Street. Modern and controversial with Graham Sutherland's huge tapestry, John Piper's coloured baptistry window and (outside) Jacob Epstein's monolithic *St Michael.*

Lady Godiva equestrian statue next door to main shopping area; **Museum of British Road Transport,** St Agnes Lane (closed Mon. — Thur. in winter); medieval **Guildhall;** 16th-century **Ford's Hospital;** and replica medieval thoroughfare of **Spon Street.**

A46 Coventry M69 Leicester

3m(4.8km) to J3

A46 Coventry (E) M69 Leicester M1 (North)

8m(11.2km)

A426 M1 (North) Rugby Lutterworth

A426 Rugby

3m(4.8km) to M1 (J19)

Coventry's important historical sights, surviving devastating air-raid of Nov. 1940, are mixed with good-looking modern architecture and landscaping inside an elevated ring road.

7m (11km) S on A46 and A427 near Binley
Coombe Abbey
Elizabethan mansion of spreading gables and chimneys; serpentine lake; well-stocked bird garden (garrulous mynahs, friendly vultures, tame falcons, penguins).

M6: *3-6*

JUNCTION 3
5m (8km) S on A444
Coventry See Junction 2

JUNCTION 4

2½m (4km) S on A446
**National Exhibition
Centre** See M42
Junction 3

5m (8km) SE on A446 and
A45
Meriden Oak tree on
village green marks
reputed centre of
England; **Cyclists'
Memorial.**

4m (6.5km) N on A446
and E (unclassified) from
Coleshill
Maxstoke Castle
Richard III slept here
before his death at
Bosworth; small
museum; 2m (3km) S is
**Maxstoke Abbey
Gatehouse**, equally
evocative of era of civil
wars in England.

JUNCTION 6

Aston Expressway,
designated **A38(M),**
leads straight to
Queensway and
Corporation Street in
the centre of
Birmingham.

BIRMINGHAM
2m (3km) S on A38(M)

Principal city-centre
feature is **Bull Ring,**
formerly a huddle of
market stalls on a
slippery slope, now an
immense shopping and
commercial complex on
several levels; big

108

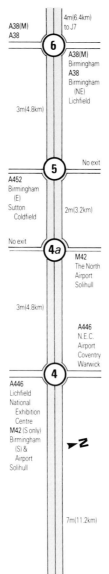

carparks, pedestrian-
only thoroughfares.
Corporation Art Gallery
has best collection of
pre-Raphaelite Paintings
anywhere (Burne-Jones
and David Cox were
local men); outstanding
William Morris
windows, designed by
Burne-Jones, in **St
Philip's Cathedral,** off
Colmore Row;
outstanding **Science and
Industry Museum,**
Newhall Street near
Victoria Square;
enshrines citizens'
involvement with heavy
and miscellaneous
engineering from early
days of steam.

4m (7km) E from city
centre on A45

Blakesley Hall, Yardley.
Timbered Elizabethan
farmhouse with folk
museum.

3m (5km) S of city centre
**Barber Institute of Fine
Arts,** Birmingham
University, Edgbaston.
Wide range of
masterpieces including
Bellini, Rembrandt,
della Robbia, Turner,
Gauguin and Rodin.

4½m (7km) S off A38

Cadbury's

**Cadbury's Chocolate
Factory,** Bournville.
Factory of 1879 in
garden suburb built by
Cadburys for their
employees; fine carillon
of bells in **Day School;**
medieval **Selly Manor**
brought in from country
and re-erected; factory
tours by prior request.

JUNCTION 7

½m (1km) N off A34 in Great Barr
Bishop Asbury's Cottage Boyhood home of first American bishop; elegant 18th-century furnishings. Closed Sun.

JUNCTION 9

LICHFIELD
12m (19km) N on Walsall ring road and A461

Three graceful sister-spires, the 'Ladies of the Vale', rise above **St Chad's Cathedral** — not the biggest in Britain by any means, but the only one with 3 spires; Flemish glass in Lady Chapel greatly prized; walkway on roof. Local history, especially Civil War involvement, in **Heritage Centre,** St Mary's. Dr Johnson memorabilia at his birthplace opposite market place, now

Samuel Johnson Birthplace Museum. Small town in which ecclesiastical calm struggles with busy traffic, especially Mon. (cattle market) and weekends. **Angel Croft hotel,** Beacon Street; 13

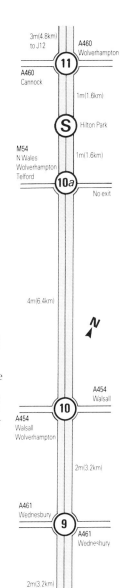

3m(4.8km) to J12 — A460 Wolverhampton

11

A460 Cannock

1m(1.6km)

S Hilton Park

M54
N Wales
Wolverhampton
Telford

1m(1.6km)

10a No exit

4m(6.4km)

A454 Walsall

10

A454 Walsall Wolverhampton

2m(3.2km)

A461 Wednesbury

9 A461 Wednesbury

2m(3.2km)

M5 The S West Birmingham W Bromwich

8

M5

2m(3.2km)

A34 Birmingham (N) Walsall

7

4m(6.4km) to J6 — A34 Birmingham (N&NE)

---

rooms; pleasantly old-fashioned. Tel: (0543) 258737.

JUNCTION 10

10m (16km) NE via Walsall on A461
Lichfield. See Junction 9

JUNCTION 11

10m (16km) NE via Cannock on A460
Large area of heath, bracken and woodland, scarred at S end with colliery workings, peaceful on minor roads N. **Great War Motor and Foot Trail** takes in German Cemetery (victims of post-1918 'flu epidemic), 'Tackeroo' military railway and other army remains. Pleasant walks from Ladyhill and Penkridge Bank carparks; sandy trail through hill and valley, with good picnic spots, from Brocton and Milford Common.

8m (13km) E on A460 and A5

Chasewater Leisure Park Watersports centre with go-kart track, greyhound circuit and miniature railway.

M6: *12-13*

JUNCTION 12

8½m (13.5km) W on A5

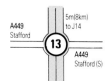

Weston Park, Weston-
under-Lizard. The
Lizard is a low-backed
hill over which the A5
Watling Street goes
ruler-straight in Roman
fashion. The Hall (Earl
of Bradford), 17th-
century, has good
portraits, including
Holbeins and
Gainsboroughs;
Aubusson and Gobelin
tapestries; Capability
Brown deerpark with
massive elms and
beeches; nature and
architectural trails;
playground, miniature
steam railway. Open
weekends spring and
autumn, daily in
summer.

A449
Stafford

5m(8km)
to J14

13

A449
Stafford (S)

JUNCTION 13

*3m (5km) E via Brocton on
gravel tracks*
Access to most
picturesque parts of
Cannock Chase. See
Junction 11

*6m (9.5km) E via Brocton
and Milford, crossing
A513*

Shugborough Hall (Earl
of Lichfield). Houses
Staffordshire County
Museum; at Home Farm
an impressive collection
of agricultural
machinery, near-extinct
breeds of cattle, sheep
and pigs; Hall has few
noteworthy treasures.
Closed in winter.

*1m (1.5km) NW of
Shugborough*
Tixall Hall Gatehouse
Tudor gatehouse, noble
in decay, all alone in a
field; with nearby **Bottle
Lodge** (chimney is the
cork) recalls vanished
Tixall Hall, where Mary
Queen of Scots was held
prisoner. 1m (1.5km) E
on edge of
Shugborough Park at
Great Haywood is a
highly photogenic
Packhorse Bridge on the
rippling, tree-shrouded
Trent.

N

6m(9.6km)

A5
Telford
Cannock
Wolverhampton

12

A5
Telford

3m(4.8)
to J11

M6: *14-15*

JUNCTION 14

*3½m (5.5km) NW via
Great Bridgeford off A5013*

Izaak Walton's Cottage,
Shallowford. Simple
little thatched cottage
near hamlet of Norton
Bridge, claimed as the
Compleat Angler's
home (he was born at
Stafford); period
furnishings, cottage
herb garden for growing
ingredients Walton
prescribed for dressing
fish, tea and coffee
available. Closed
Mon.-Wed.

*6m (9.5km) via Great
Bridgeford on B5405.*
Yew Tree Inn, Ranton.
Sophisticated cuisine at
moderate prices in a
drowsy little hamlet.
Tel: Seighford 278.

JUNCTION 15

*1½m (2km) E and S on
A34*

Trentham Gardens Old-
established leisure park

in 800 acres (323
hectares) of woodland
on the estate of former
Dukes of Sutherland;
rose, rock and Italian
gardens; miniature
railway and boating in
summer; bars,
restaurants, a large
caravan park also.

*4m (7km) E and S on A34
and E (signposted)*

**Wedgwood Visitor
Centre,** Barlaston.
Displays of Jasper ware
and bone china at
Wedgwood factory;
refreshment lounge,
shop.

STOKE-UPON-TRENT
3m (5km) E on A500
Factory tours of
renowned china firms
at Royal Doulton, Nile
Street, Burslem; Spode
of City Road, Stoke;
Minton, London Road,
Stoke; and others.

**Gladstone Pottery
Museum** in old potbank
on Uttoxeter Road,
Longton; **Lowen
Gallery,** Hartshill Road
on A52, shows modern
ceramics and gifts.

Map labels: 7m(11.2km) to J16 · Keele · S · 3m(4.8km) · A500 Stoke (S) Stone Eccleshall · 15 · A500 Stoke-on-Trent Newcastle · N · 11m(17.6km) · A34 Eccleshall Stone Stafford (N) · 14 · A34 Stafford (N) · 5m(8km) to J13

M6: *16-18*

JUNCTION 16

NANTWICH
8m (13km) E on A500 and W on A52 (crossing motorway)

Old salt town, black-and-white houses all askew; majestic **Parish Church; Manor House Mews,** delightful shopping development; **Churche's Mansion,** fine Tudor town house.

2m (3km) SE of Nantwich on A51
Stapeley Water Gardens
Big bustling park; tropical fish, small sharks; aquatic effects and amusements.

2m (3km) N of Nantwich on B5074
Rookery Hall Hotel,
Worleston. Smart restaurant in big country house; expensive. Tel: Nantwich 626866.

7m (11km) E on A500 and N via Tunstall on A527

Chatterley-Whitfield Mining Museum Large mine reopened for underground tours. Closed Sat. in winter.

JUNCTION 17

5m (8km) E on A534 and A34
Little Moreton Hall, near Congleton. Stunningly evocative;

112

7m(11.2km) to services

A54 Holmes Chapel Middlewich

18

A54 Holmes Chapel Middlewich Northwich Chester

4m(6.4km)

N

A534 Sandbach Crewe Congleton

17

A534 Congleton Sandbach Crewe

1m(1.6km)

S Sandbach

5m(8km)

A500 Newcastle Stoke-on-Trent

16

A500 Stoke Kidsgrove

7m(11.2km) to services

knot garden; home-baked teas. Closed in winter.

JUNCTION 18

4m (6.5km) E via Holmes Chapel on A535

Jodrell Bank Visitor centre; giant telescope and a smaller one; planetarium; restaurant. Closed Nov.-Feb.

7m (11km) E on A535 and minor road (signposted)
Capesthorne Hall, Siddington. Imposing early-Georgian hall on older foundations; Bromley-Davenports have lived there since Norman Conquest; portraits, sculptures, Colonial-style furniture; gardens, chapel, lake, woodland trail; garden restaurant. Closed in winter.

10m (16km) E on A535 and B5392

Gawsworth Hall, Gawsworth. 15th-century manor, low-built; perhaps most beautiful half-timbered house in a region which bristles with them; **showplace village** adjoining; Mary Fitton, Shakespeare's 'Dark Lady', lived here.

JUNCTION 19

KNUTSFORD
3m (5km) E on A50
Immortalized by Mrs
Gaskell as 'Cranford',
still looks the part,
though shaken by
juggernaut lorries. **La
Belle Epoque
restaurant,** King Street,
gourmet French menus
and art-nouveau décor.
Tel: Knutsford 3060.

*3m (5km) E on A556 and
A5034*

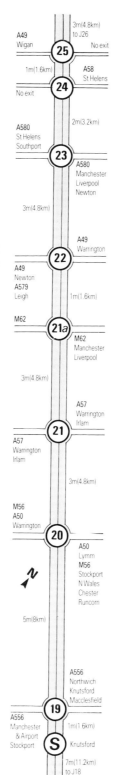

Tatton Park Palladian
house and great park;
Japanese garden; home
farm; tenants' hall is a
museum of rural relics;
sailing, bathing, fishing
on lake; refreshments.

4½m (7km) W off B5391
Arley Hall See M56
Junction 10

6m (10km) W on A556
Salt Museum, London
Road, Northwich. Salty
matters from down the
ages in this metropolis
of the industry; slide
show. Closed Sun. in
winter.

JUNCTION 20
6m (10km) E on A50
Tatton Park See
Junction 19

JUNCTION 21
*3m (5km) W to Padgate
and E on A574, crossing
motorway*
Risley Moss See M62
Junction 11

JUNCTION 23

*4m (6.5km) E on A580 and
A572*

Pennington Flash A
new country park round
lake; some bird species
rehabilitated; plants and
butterflies; rudimentary
at present.

5m (8km) W on A58
**Pilkington Glass
Museum,** St Helens.
See M57, junction with
A57

JUNCTION 25

*3½m (5.5km) E on
motorway spur and A49*

Wigan Pier Grand
Heritage Complex 'The
Way We Were' beside
canal banks and genuine
but minuscule Wigan
Pier. Concert hall,
waterbuses; **Orwell Inn**
(tel. Wigan 323034)
authentic hostelry
recommended for meals
and snacks; shop;
Waterway Gardens;
steam-driven
Trencherfield Mill,
ropewalk, other
resuscitated trades and
crafts; easy carparking
on Wallgate, opposite
Heritage Complex.

M6: 26-29

JUNCTION 26
3m (5km) E on A577 and A49
Wigan Pier Alternative access via Wigan. See Junction 25

JUNCTION 27

4m (6.5km) W on A5209 and N on B5250
Camelot, Park Hall. Lively and inventive theme park/funfair/mini-Disneyworld; garden centre, caravan park; crafts and antiques fairs every Sun.; record collectors' bazaar.

11m (18km) W on A5209 and B5264

Rufford Old Hall, Rufford. Remarkable Jacobean timber-framed house with medieval Great Hall; gardens, dogs not excluded; shop and tearoom. Closed in winter.

12m (19km) W and N on A5209 and A59

Martin Mere Wildfowl Trust refuge for native and migrant birds; flamingoes, rare geese and swans; observation posts.

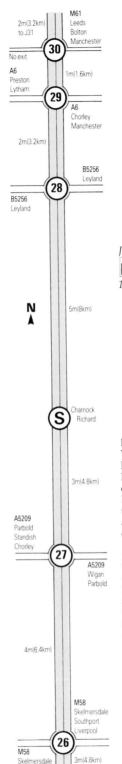

N

2m(3.2km) to J31	M61 Leeds Bolton Manchester
No exit	**30**
A6 Preston Lytham	**29** 1m(1.6km)
	A6 Chorley Manchester
2m(3.2km)	
	B5256 Leyland
B5256 Leyland	**28**
	5m(8km)
	S Charnock Richard
	3m(4.8km)
A5209 Parbold Standish Chorley	**27**
	A5209 Wigan Parbold
4m(6.4km)	
	M58 Skelmersdale Southport Liverpool
M58 Skelmersdale Southport	**26** 3m(4.8km) to J25

JUNCTION 28

1m (1.5km) W

British Commercial Vehicle Museum in King Street, Leyland Many vehicular curiosities; home of Leyland buses and trucks since 1896; open all summer, weekends only in winter.

1m (1.5km) W
Worden Hall Craft Centre, in Worden Park, Leyland. Potters, saddlers, painters, woodworkers, enamellers at work in converted country house; forge, maze, trim trail, the inevitable miniature railway; coffee shop.

JUNCTION 29
2m (3km) W off A49 (crossing motorway twice)
Alternative access to **British Commercial Vehicle Museum,** Leyland. See Junction 28

JUNCTION 31

1m (1.5km) W on A59
Duke of Lancaster's Own Yeomanry Museum in Stanley Street, Preston; history, chiefly pictorial, of Britain's oldest yeomanry regiment.

4m (7.5km) E on A59 and A677
Samlesbury Hall Hoary mansion, mullioned and many-gabled, enjoying new lease of life with arts/crafts exhibitions and sales. Closed Mon.

9m (14.5km) E on A59 and minor road across Ribble (signposted)

Ribchester Roman station from 80AD; nothing much *in situ* but small museum has Roman soldier's tombstone and copy of well-known Ribchester Helmet (original in British Museum).

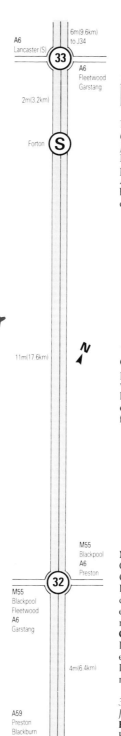

JUNCTION 33

LANCASTER
6m (10km) W and N to Junction 33A and A6
Interesting town with parking problems; **Ashton Memorial,** a baroque Taj Mahal, dominates skyline;

Castle; stern structure, partly prison, partly visitable in summer; little **Dockland** on Lune estuary, with boats and fishing;

Maritime Museum, Custom House, St George's Quay, recalls Lancaster's venerable deep-sea links; some exquisite sailing-ship models; **Museum of Childhood,** Judge's Lodging, Church Street, emphasis on Victoriana. Labyrinthine streets, many antique shops.

3m (5km) W and S via Junction 33A and A6
Foxholes hotel, Bay Horse, Forton. Quiet country house; 10 spacious rooms; inexpensive. Tel: (0524) 791237.

M6: 34-35

4m(6.4km) to J36

JUNCTION 34

2m (3km) W on A683
Lancaster Alternative access. See Junction 33

10m (16km) W via Lancaster and B5273
Heysham No. 1 Nuclear Power Station Britain's largest nuclear complex; tight security, but you can climb the observation tower; closed in winter.

7m (11km) E on A683

Hornby and **Lune Valley.** Castle and village strikingly poised over the Lune. Footpaths and cycleways follow the river and A683 all the way, touching at **Caton** (2m (3km) from junction) and **Brookhouse** (3m(5km)), 2 attractive villages; also horseshoe bend called **Crook o' Lune** near Caton, painted by Turner. Numerous picnic sites.

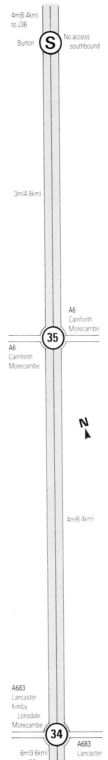

Burton (S) No access southbound

3m(4.8km)

A6 Carnforth Morecambe

(35)

A6 Carnforth Morecambe

N

4m(6.4km)

A683 Lancaster Kirkby Lonsdale Morecambe

(34)
A683 Lancaster

6m(9.6km) to J33

JUNCTION 35

1½m (2km) W and S via Exit 35A and A6

Steamtown, Warton Road, Carnforth. Might and majesty of 1930s express locomotives assembled in former railway yards; gift shop, collectors' corner, café. Closed in winter.

3m (5km) W and N via Exit 35A and A6
Leighton Hall, Yealand Conyers. White castellated hall associated with Gillows, respected cabinet-making family; furniture, clocks, figurines; falconry displays. Closed in winter.

SILVERDALE
5m (8km) W via Junction 35A to minor road (signposted)
Pleasant hamlet scattered amid scrub and woodland on rocky coast; caves; author Mrs Gaskell lived at **Gibraltar Cottage.** Opposite, prestigious

Wolf House Gallery in Georgian farmhouse; textile workshops and artists' studios in outbuildings; coffee room; bicycles for hire. Worth the detour.

JUNCTION 36

4m (6.5km) W on A591 and A6.

Levens Hall, Levens Bridge. Elizabethan hall (plasterwork, panelling) in just the right environment; garden famous for its delightful topiary work.

5m (8km) NW on A591 near Kendal

Sizergh Castle Home of venerable Strickland family; toy-fort-like but genuine enough, furnished with Jacobean treasures; mature garden noted for rock plants, hardy ferns and dwarf conifers. Closed Tue., Fri. and Sat. and all winter.

7m (11km) E on A65

Eaveslea Country House restaurant, New Road, Kirkby Lonsdale. Tel: (0468) 71209. Ample wholesome food, moderate prices; in a historic Luneside market town with rambling

alleyways, medieval church and 'devil's bridge'.

KENDAL

6m (9.5km) NW on A65

The Brewery, Highgate. Arts complex (exhibitions, theatre, jazz, mime, lunchtime concerts in summer) in architecturally interesting old brewery;

9m(14.4km) to J38

A684 Kendal Sedbergh

(37)

A684 Kendal Sedbergh

1m(1.6km)

No access northbound **(S)** Killington Lake

7m(11.2km)

A591 S Lakes Kendal Barrow A65 Skipton Kirkby Lonsdale

(36)

A65 A591

4m(6.4km) to J35

---

a fairly basic restaurant. **John Farrer,** Stricklandgate. Tea and coffee merchants; service, stock and premises recall a Jane-Austenish yesterday. **Castle Dairy restaurant,** Wildman Street; regional delicacies at reasonable prices. Tel: (0539) 211700.

JUNCTION 37

5m (8km) W on A684

Alternative access to **Kendal.** See Junction 36

SEDBERGH

6m (9.5km) E on A684

Dour little stone-built town near confluence of turbulent trout streams; in **Weaver's Yard** the massive chimney where (they say) Bonnie Prince Charlie hid; good stained glass in **St Andrew's Church;**

Old Grammar School, formerly the well-known Sedbergh School and now the school library; caving instruction with experts (summer only) at **Whernside,** just out of town.

M6: 38-39

JUNCTION 38

APPLEBY
13m (21km) NE on B6260

Quiet little grey town of
the fells, still clinging to
old dignity of a county
town and assize centre;
castle with Norman
keep, ditch and rampart
is centre for Rare Breeds
Survival Trust; excellent
walking and touring
centre. **Royal Oak Inn
restaurant,** Bongate;
beams, oak panels; good
fresh food and very
reasonable prices. Tel:
(0930) 51463.

KIRKBY STEPHEN
12m (19km) E on A685

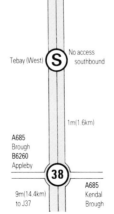

Like Appleby (above), a
good-looking self-
sufficient little town,
calm and sleepy except
on days of ram sales and
horse and pony fairs
(end Sept.). 3m (5km) S
of Kirkby Stephen on
B6259 stands **Pendragon
Castle,** wreck of a
powerful Clifford
fortress, reputed
stronghold of Uther
Pendragon in Arthurian
legend; in swirling mist
it certainly sets the

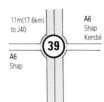

11m(17.6km)
to J40

A6
Shap
Kendal

39

A6
Shap

imagination working;
must get landowner's
permission to enter.

JUNCTION 39

3m (5km) W and N on A6
Shap Abbey, near Shap.
Central tower almost
intact; a short distance
W, on edge of Shap
village, **standing stones,**
of which only the
curiously-named
Goggleby is worth the
stroll.

5m(8km)

Tebay (West) **S** No access
southbound

1m(1.6km)

A685
Brough
B6260
Appleby

38

9m(14.4km)
to J37

A685
Kendal
Brough

JUNCTION 40

3m (5km) W on A66 and A592

Dalemain Large lived-in stately home with accretions from every architectural period since Saxon times; spacious park accommodates 2 country museums, a regimental museum (Westmorland and Cumberland yeomanry) and a children's playground. Closed in winter.

5m (8km) S off A6 (W of motorway)

Lowther Park, Askham. Big brash entertainment park laid out under gaze of pseudo-medieval **Lowther Castle.**

2m (3km) E off A6

Brougham Castle Cannot compete with others in this hotbed of castles and stately homes, but its four-square 12th-century tower set in splendid isolation makes a refreshing change.

7m (11km) E on A66
Acorn Bank, Temple Sowerby. Well-known National Trust garden; roses, flowering trees, wildflowers best in spring; medicinal and culinary herbs in

profusion. Closed Nov.-Mar.

3m (5km) SW off A592
Four Bears in churchyard at Dacre; comical stone monuments at each corner of church; ancient and obscure origin.

8m (13km) SW on A66 and A592
Leeming-on-Ullswater hotel On lake shore near Watermillock; 25 luxurious rooms, superior restaurant; tranquil, fastidious, expensive. Tel: (08536) 444.

JUNCTION 41

5m (8km) W on B5305
Hutton-in-the-Forest Castle (Lord Inglewood). Mock-Gothic, tapestries, legend of King Arthur; pretty forest walk; house closed in winter.

Map labels:

8m(12.8km) to services

B5305 Wigton

41

B5305 Wigton

3m(4.8km)

A66 N Lakes Penrith Keswick

40

A66 Penrith Keswick Brough

11m(17.6km) to J39

119

JUNCTION 42

WETHERAL
4m (6.5km) E on B6263
Corby Castle Gardens only, plus a delightful footpath along river Eden. Closed in winter.

Crown hotel; 50 rooms; first-class restaurant, sophisticated cuisine for an old-fashioned village; fairly expensive. Tel: (0228) 61888.

CARLISLE
4m (6.5km) W on A6
Round-towered **Citadel** near railway station;

Castle, N end of town, redolent of stormy Border affrays; small but handsome **Cathedral;** on historic thoroughfare Scotch Street/English Street; **The Lanes,** new shopping and exhibitions area; off Cecil Street, S end, **Antique and Craft Centre,** 12 little craft, jewelry and fashion shops with smart **Penny Farthing** snack bar.

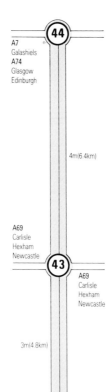

A7 Galashiels
A74 Glasgow Edinburgh

4m(6.4km)

A69 Carlisle Hexham Newcastle

A69 Carlisle Hexham Newcastle

3m(4.8km)

A6 Carlisle

A6 Carlisle

5m(8km)

Southwaite

8m(12.8km) to J41

JUNCTION 43

2m (3km) W on A69
Carlisle See Junction 42

BRAMPTON
8m (13km) NE on A69
Characteristic hill village within walking distance

of **Hadrian's Wall. Farlam Hall hotel,** converted farmhouse; restaurant patronized by discerning locals; moderate to expensive. Tel: (069 76) 234. Nearby are 2 medieval survivals well worth looking at:

Lanercost Priory, partly restored; and **Naworth Castle** (Earl of Carlisle), with fine tapestries, armour and heraldic carvings.

JUNCTION 44

3m (5km) S on A7
Carlisle See Junction 42

10m (16km) NW on A74
Gretna Green At **Old Blacksmith's,** where marriages illegal in England could be solemnized under Scots law, mock ceremonies are performed as entertainment for coach parties.

M602:

Eccles to Manchester, 4½m (7km)

All motorways lead to Manchester — or so it appears to the motorist in the north-west. The M602, however, is the only motorway to penetrate Manchester's heart. It provides a clear run from the M62 via Salford. Junctions are unnumbered (numbered here in brackets). There is one intermediate junction. Places of interest in west or west-central Manchester are most accessible from this route.

JUNCTION (2)

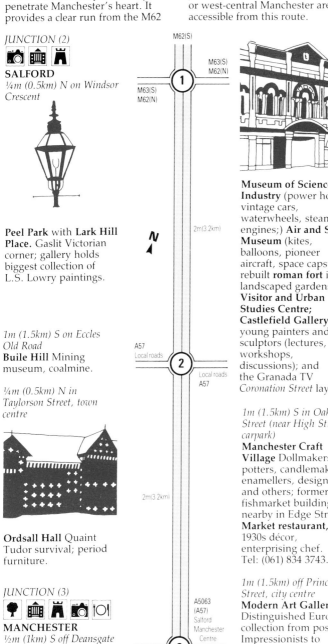

SALFORD
¼m (0.5km) N on Windsor Crescent

Peel Park with **Lark Hill Place.** Gaslit Victorian corner; gallery holds biggest collection of L.S. Lowry paintings.

1m (1.5km) S on Eccles Old Road
Buile Hill Mining museum, coalmine.

¼m (0.5km) N in Taylorson Street, town centre

Ordsall Hall Quaint Tudor survival; period furniture.

JUNCTION (3)

MANCHESTER
½m (1km) S off Deansgate
Castlefield Britain's first urban heritage park. Within its bounds are

M62(S)

M63(S)
M62(N)

M63(S)
M62(N)

2m(3.2km)

A57
Local roads

Local roads
A57

2m(3.2km)

A5063
(A57)
Salford
Manchester
Centre

Museum of Science and Industry (power house, vintage cars, waterwheels, steam engines;) **Air and Space Museum** (kites, balloons, pioneer aircraft, space capsules); rebuilt **roman fort** in landscaped gardens; **Visitor and Urban Studies Centre; Castlefield Gallery** for young painters and sculptors (lectures, workshops, discussions); and the Granada TV *Coronation Street* layout.

1m (1.5km) S in Oak Street (near High Street carpark)
Manchester Craft Village Dollmakers, potters, candlemakers, enamellers, designers and others; former fishmarket building; nearby in Edge Street, **Market restaurant,** 1930s décor, enterprising chef. Tel: (061) 834 3743.

1m (1.5km) off Princess Street, city centre
Modern Art Gallery Distinguished European collection from post-Impressionists to Hockney; also Moore, Hepworth, Epstein sculptures.

121

M606:

Spenborough to Bradford, 3m (5km)

This spur from the M62 serves only Bradford, arriving with only one intermediate junction to within 2m (3km) of the city centre. The terminal junction (here numbered in brackets) is actually unnumbered.

JUNCTION (1)

BRADFORD
2m (3km) N on A641

A6036
A6177
Bradford Ring Road
A641
City Centre

A proud city now boasting some striking city-centre architecture. Metropolis of visual science and technology, e.g. **National Museum of Photography, Film and Television,** Prince's View (cinema nostalgia, all the latest in 3D spectaculars, biggest screen in Britain); and **Colour Museum,** Grattan Road, NW of centre (brilliant displays and demonstrations of colour, dyes, pigments, influence of colour on human, animal, plant life). Both highly recommended.

SHIPLEY

4m (6.5km) N via Bradford on A641 and A6037

Waterbus, summer only, to Bingley on atmospheric 4m (6.5km) stretch of Leeds and Liverpool Canal. At Bingley, **Five Rise Locks,** a triumph of old-time canal technology.

11m (17.5km) W from Bradford on slowish moorland road B6144

Brontë Parsonage, Haworth. Now the Brontë Museum with intimate relics of Patrick, Branwell, Emily, Charlotte and Anne. Excellent value. Through Haworth station runs 4m (6.5km) **steam passenger railway** between Oxenhope and Keighley on Keighley and Worth Valley line. Bank holidays and summer weekends only.

8m (13km) N from Bradford on A6037 and A6038
Harry Ramsden's, White Cross, Guiseley. Famous fish-and-chip shop, biggest in the world. Other meals available too in these astoundingly opulent chandeliered and deep-pile-carpeted rooms. Efficient service and very reasonable prices.

1m(1.6km)

Bierley
Bierley
1½m(2.4km) to M62 (J26)

M61:

Manchester to Preston, 22m (35km)

Through its junction with the M6 on the outskirts of Preston, this motorway serves traffic between Manchester and Carlisle and beyond. It is an exceptionally busy route, lined with the industrial and one-time cotton-spinning towns of the Greater Manchester conurbation for the first half of the journey. Around Junction 6 it emerges into more open country, with the steep wall of the Pennines to the east; and for 4m (7km) it borders the long narrow reservoir of Rivington (Liverpool Waterworks). Then comes the gradual descent to the valley of the Ribble, with sweeping views of the Forest of Bowland (not woodland but moorland) to the north and, close at hand, the manufacturing town of Preston.

The M61's first junction is on the M62 transpennine motorway and its last, Junction 9, is on the M6. Of the intermediate junctions, 7 has not yet been built.

JUNCTION 2

BOLTON

4m (6.5km) N via Junction 3 and A666.

Not a pretty town, but a place of character; **Museum and Art Gallery** next to Town Hall contains some outstanding English watercolours and recent acquisitions of *avant-garde* type, e.g. Edward Burra's *Bird Women: Duennas*. Two antique mansions antedate the

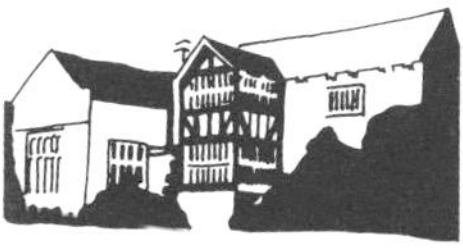

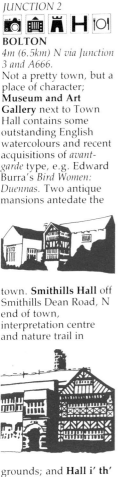

town. **Smithills Hall** off Smithills Dean Road, N end of town, interpretation centre and nature trail in

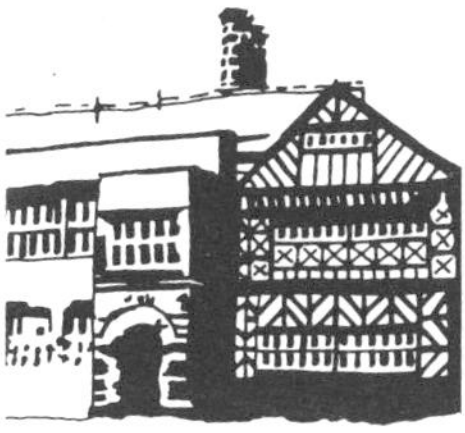

grounds; and **Hall i' th' Wood** off Crompton Way (A58), superbly ornate half-timbered manor furnished in 17th-century style; both houses picturesque, the latter having its place in history too as the former home of Samuel Crompton, inventor of cotton-spinning machinery.

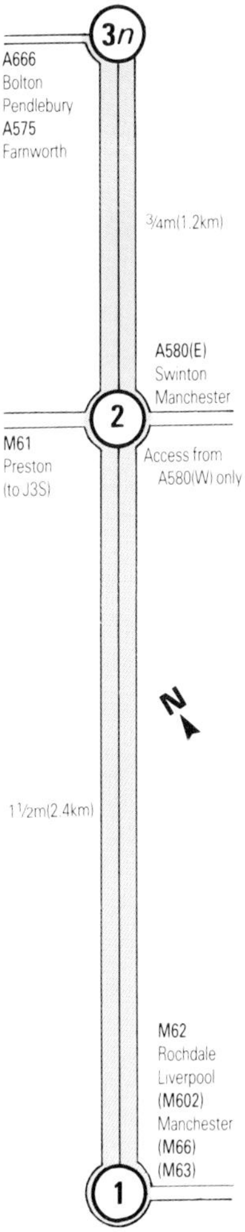
3n
A666
Bolton
Pendlebury
A575
Farnworth
¾m(1.2km)
A580(E)
Swinton
Manchester
2
M61
Preston
(to J3S)
Access from
A580(W) only
N
1½m(2.4km)
M62
Rochdale
Liverpool
(M602)
Manchester
(M66)
(M63)
1

11m (19km) via Bolton and A676

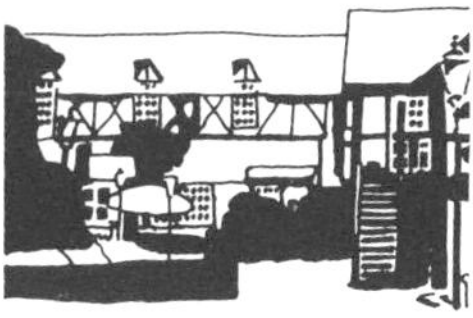

Last Drop Village, Bromley Cross. Group of farm buildings on a moorland slope, transformed into rather self-conscious tourist amenity; **luxury hotel** with 80 rooms, sauna, jacuzzi etc.; **Restaurant on the Hill, Stocks restaurant; Drop Inn** olde-worlde pub; teashop, crafts and antiques. Not everyone's cup of tea but a novelty for central Lancashire. Site of **Northwest Regional Tourist Board.**

M61: 4-8

JUNCTION 4

4½m (7km) S across A6 and A580 to A575, crossing M63

Worsley Old Hall
Graceful 16th-century manor house with spreading black-and-white wings; home of Elizabethan ancestor of canal-building Duke of Bridgewater; medieval banquets every evening (must book). Tel: (061) 799 5015.

JUNCTION 5

3m (5km) NE on A58 and A6140
Bolton See Junction 2
7m (11km) NE on A58 and A676
Last Drop Village See Junction 2

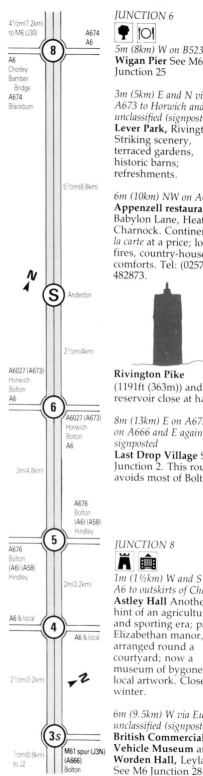

4½m(7.2km) to M6 (J30)

A674
A6

8

A6
Chorley
Bamber
Bridge
A674
Blackburn

5½m(8.8km)

N

S Anderton

2½m(4km)

A6027 (A673)
Horwich
Bolton
A6

6

A6027 (A673)
Horwich
Bolton
A6

3m(4.8km)

A676
Bolton
(A6) (A58)
Hindley

5

A676
Bolton
(A6) (A58)
Hindley

2m(3.2km)

A6 & local

4

A6 & local

2½m(3.2km)

Z

3s

½m(0.8km)
to J2

M61 spur (J3N)
(A666)
Bolton

JUNCTION 6

5m (8km) W on B5238
Wigan Pier See M6 Junction 25

3m (5km) E and N via A673 to Horwich and N unclassified (signposted)
Lever Park, Rivington. Striking scenery, terraced gardens, historic barns; refreshments.

6m (10km) NW on A6
Appenzell restaurant, Babylon Lane, Heath Charnock. Continental *à la carte* at a price; log fires, country-house comforts. Tel: (0257) 482873.

Rivington Pike
(1191ft (363m)) and reservoir close at hand.

8m (13km) E on A673, N on A666 and E again, signposted
Last Drop Village See Junction 2. This route avoids most of Bolton.

JUNCTION 8

1m (1½km) W and S on A6 to outskirts of Chorley
Astley Hall Another hint of an agricultural and sporting era; partly Elizabethan manor, arranged round a courtyard; now a museum of bygones and local artwork. Closed in winter.

6m (9.5km) W via Euxton, unclassified (signposted)
British Commercial Vehicle Museum and **Worden Hall**, Leyland. See M6 Junction 28

M62: Liverpool
to North Cave, 108m (173km)

Though not quite complete from coast to coast, the M62 is Britain's principal west-east motorway. Much of the route carries heavy traffic, for it threads the sprawling industrial towns and cities of Lancashire and Yorkshire, the milltowns of cotton and wool, the heavy-engineering and coalmining centres. It links the north country's great cities — Liverpool, Manchester and Leeds — and almost every notable manufacturing town, from Warrington to Wakefield, lies on or near its route. End to end it makes a journey through the workshop of England and various aspects of industry and commerce are explained in the numerous museums, theme parks and restored factories along the way.

At present the M62 begins at Junction 4 on the edge of Liverpool and ends some 15m (24km) short of Hull.

JUNCTION 4

LIVERPOOL
1m (1.5km) W on Queen's Drive and West Derby Road
A city full of exciting things and most of them easily reached from this

junction. The **Anglican** and ultra-modern **Metropolitan Cathedrals** are at either end of Hope Street; the **Walker Art Gallery** has world-renowned collection of European art from medieval to modern; Stubbs, Turner, Millais, Holman

Hunt; and the **County Museums** with **Planetarium** are in William Brown Street;

A5080 Huyton

3m(4.8km) to J6

(5)

A5080 Knotty Ash Huyton

Z◄

1m(1.6km)

A5058 Ring Rd N Bootle Docks:Ferries Ring Road S Airport Widnes
A5080 City Centre Car Ferries Birkenhead Wallasey

(4)

---

also fine old **Bluecoat Chambers** is in School Lane (adjoining main shops) with arts, crafts, theatre and bistro. Contemporary Liverpool offers **Beatle City,** Seel Street (to be moved — see Junction 5); **Merseyside Maritime Museum** at the Pierhead

and **Albert Dock Village** (craft fairs, busking, lunchtime theatre) alongside; and

Lark Lane Motor Museum (cheerfully nostalgic, tearoom) in Hesketh Street. **Lau's restaurant,** Ullet Road, is famous for Chinese cooking which Liverpool's large Chinese population rates highly.

M62: 5-19

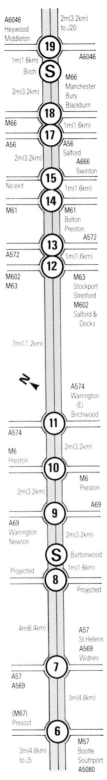

JUNCTION 5

3m (5km) S on A562 and A561

Transworld Festival Gardens Horticulture and botany of China, India, Turkey and elsewhere; children's magic garden; **Beatle City** will be here in 1987; leisure parks and riverfront walks.

3½m (5.5km) S on A562 and A561

Speke Hall Lovely half-timbered Tudor manorhouse with gardens; refreshments.

JUNCTION 7

3½m (5.5km) S on A569 signposted Widnes
Halton Museum, Alforde Street, Widnes (behind Old Town Hall). Old and new in the glass, chemicals, plastics and textiles industries.

JUNCTION 11

1½m (2.5km) S on A574 at Ordnance Avenue, Birchwood
Risley Moss Rather grey area of reclaimed bog and peatmoss; ponds, wildlife observation tower; visitor centre and guided walks.

JUNCTION 12
2m (3km) E on M602
Salford See M602 Junction (2)

5m (8km) E on M602
Manchester See M602 Junction (3)

JUNCTION 13

½m (1km) E on A572
Worsley A green and half-timbered residential suburb of Greater Manchester; site of ancient **Bridgewater Canal** with a curious aqueduct.

JUNCTION 17

1m (1½km) S on A56

Heaton Hall and Park One of Manchester's major country-park attractions; small admission charge to house, a fine Palladian building with unusual décor; oriental porcelains and prints; large shady park with animals and a tramway museum with passenger-carrying veteran tram. **Village Squash Club and hotel,** Sedgley Park, Prestwick; 28 rooms; upper price range. Tel: (061) 798 8905.

JUNCTION 19

3½m (5.5km) S to Cheetham Hill, off A664

Manchester Museum of Transport Public service vehicles from Manchester district, from horse-drawn omnibuses to present day; bookshop and cafeteria.

JUNCTION 20
3½m (6km) N on
A627(M) and A58.
Toad Lane Museum,
Rochdale. See A627(M)

JUNCTION 21

2m (3km) N on B6226
**Hollingworth Lake
Country Park** Sizeable
crescent of water;
surrounding land
reclaimed from
industry; boating,
walking, birdwatching,
picnicking; original
Victorian promenade
under reconstruction.

*1m (1.5km) beyond
Hollingworth, over
Rochdale Canal*

**Littleborough Coach
House** Of considerable
historic and architectural
value; being renovated
and prepared as
heritage centre; close
by, **Roman road,**
excavation pending.

JUNCTION 22

HEBDEN BRIDGE
*14m (22.5km) N on A672,
A58 and A646*

Town of characteristic
millstone grit in deep
valley of Calder river;
interesting topography
attracts tourists;
scrambling and rock-
climbing to dramatic
viewpoints; **packhorse**

bridge with adjacent
Bridge Mill,
shop/crafts/restaurant
conversion; **Clog Mill,**
still working, welcomes

visitors; **Automobilia** in
Billy Lane, Wadsworth,
purveys motor and
motor-cycle nostalgia
and has **Austrian
restaurant. Hebden
Lodge hotel,** New Road,
a high-Victorian
building, offers high-
Victorian amenities and
its restaurant,
Brindley's, is small but
select, with first-class
cuisine; excellent value
for reasonable charges.
Tel: (0422) 845272.

*10m (16km) N on A672
and A58*
Rochdale Canal at
Sowerby Bridge.
Proclaimed 'Yorkshire's
secret waterway';
newly-restored for
holiday traffic and
towpath walkers
through romantic gorges
and bleak moorland.

6m (9.5km) N on A672

Ryburn Farm Museum,
Ripponden. Equipment
and machinery evoke
harsh life of mid-
Victorian farming
community. **Over the
Bridge restaurant,**
Millfold, Ripponden.
Elegant French cuisine,
on the expensive side;
mentioned in food
guides. Tel: (0422)
823722.

7m(11.2km)
to J23

22

A672
Ripponden
Sowerby
Bridge (A58)

A672
Saddleworth

4m(6.4km)

N

A640
Milnrow
Shaw

21

A640
Milnrow
Shaw

2m(3.2km)

A627(M)
Rochdale
Oldham

20

A627(M)
Oldham
Ashton
Rochdale

2m(3.2km)
to J19

M62: 23-26

JUNCTION 23

7m (11km) SE off A640 and W on A62 and unclassified road
Golcar has **Colne Valley Museum,** textiles and clogs, in preserved row of former weavers' cottages. Weekends and bank holidays only.

JUNCTION 24

HALIFAX
4m (6.5km) N on A629

Off Market Street, town centre, **Piece Hall,** 200-year-old woollen 'piece' (lengths of cloth) emporium, now superbly restored to colonnaded dignity round its quadrangle, housing antique shops, museums and art galleries in its 315 rooms; **open-air market** Fri. and Sat. on cobbled quadrangle (over which Blondin once walked on his tightrope). **Princess hotel,** Princess Street: 50 well-furnished rooms, and **Marquee restaurant** locally renowned for regional and Continental dishes and bar lunches; ample carparking nearby. Tel: (0422) 54227.

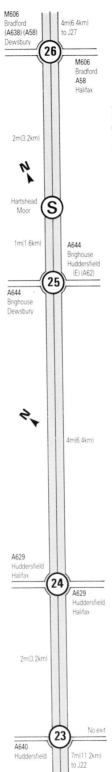

1½m (2.5km) E from Halifax on A58
Shibden Hall Delightful old black-and-white house in park; **West Yorkshire Folk Museum** in courtyard.

ALMONDBURY

6m (10km) SE off A629
Attractive moorside village with quaint houses and medieval church; legendary tower (actually Victorian) on neighbouring **Castle Hill** (1000ft (305m)) is a panoramic viewpoint.

JUNCTION 25

5m (8km) NW on A644
Alternative access to **Shibden Hall,** avoiding Halifax. See Junction 24

1m (1.5km) W on A644
Access to **Calderdale Way,** a series of linked footpaths over hill and dale W to Todmorden (total length 50m (80km)).

JUNCTION 26

5m (8km) N on M606
Bradford See M606

2m (3km) E on A58 and S on A651 (crossing and recrossing M62)

Red House, Oxford Road, Gomersal. Neat Jacobean house, appropriately furnished; has links with John Wesley and Charlotte Brontë (as 'Briarmains' in the novel *Shirley*).

JUNCTION 27

7m (11km) N on M621
Leeds See M621

3m (5km) S on A62 and A652
Oakwell Hall Country Park Another ancient stone-and-timber mansion with period furnishings and a character of its own; 'Fieldhead' in Charlotte Brontë's *Shirley*; visitor centre in park; formal gardens, arboretum, wildlife, walks, picnic area.

JUNCTION 28

3½m (5.5km) N off A653, S of Leeds
Middleton Railway, Tunstall Road. Steam trips (summer weekends only) on 1m (1.5km) of horsedrawn tramway of 1758, allegedly oldest surviving 'railway' in world; not well signposted and primarily for rail enthusiasts/historians.

JUNCTION 29
5m (8km) N on M1
Alternative access to **Leeds.** See M621

JUNCTION 30

4m (6.5km) N on A642 and W following signposts
Temple Newsam The 'Hampton Court of the North'; beautiful rosebrick Tudor-Jacobean palace lavishly furnished; Chippendale chairs, cabinets; birthplace of Lord Darnley, husband of Mary Queen of Scots; huge park with celebrated azalea and rhododendron gardens; farmyard, rare breeds of cattle; restaurant open in summer.

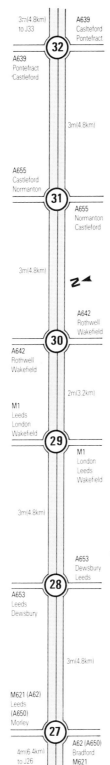

JUNCTION 31

9m (14.5km) N on A655, A656 and B1217

Lotherton Hall Aberford. Stylish Edwardian house; oriental pottery, modern ceramics, fashionwear; gardens; livestock; largest bird garden in Britain; café and restaurant.

JUNCTION 32

5½m (9km) S on A639 and A628

Nostell Priory One of Yorkshire's great houses and most splendid parks; house partly Adam; Chippendale furniture, 'Longitude' Harrison clocks (both worked there as boys); tearoom. Closed in winter.

9m (14.5km) N on A656 and B1217
Alternative access to **Lotherton Hall.** See Junction 31

M62: 33-36

JUNCTION 33

10m (16km) N on A1 and B1217
Alternative access to **Lotherton Hall.** See Junction 31

13m (21km) N on A1 and A64

Hazelwood Castle, near Bramham crossroads. Ancestral seat of Vavasours, Catholic martyrs in penal times; now a Carmelite friary; facilities for visitors, guesthouse for pilgrims.

2½m (4km) SW on A645
King's Croft Hotel, Pontefract. Peaceful Georgian house in leafy setting; 12 rooms; ample and varied menus; quite cheap. Tel: (0977) 703419.

JUNCTION 34

6½m (10.5km) NE on A19, A645 and A1041

Carlton Towers House is fussy Victorian-Gothic but it guards a rich haul of china, silver and wood carvings; priest's hole; tearoom in stables. Open Sun. and bank holidays, summer only.

9m (14.5km) N on A19 via Selby and B1223
Cawood Bright little village with some archaic brick houses and a **swing-bridge** on the

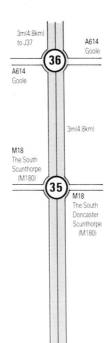

3m(4.8km) to J37

A614 Goole

36

A614 Goole

3m(4.8km)

M18 The South Scunthorpe (M180)

35

M18 The South Doncaster Scunthorpe (M180)

8m(12.8km)

A19 Doncaster Selby

34

A19 Selby Doncaster

5m(8km)

Ferrybridge services A1(N&S) Doncaster

33

Ferrybridge services A1(N&S)

3m(4.8km) to J32

Ouse; formidable 15th-century **gatehouse** is all that remains of a bishop's castle.

SELBY
7m (11km) N on A19
Attractive market town

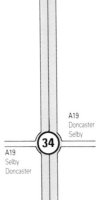

with notable **abbey,** parts dating from 1100 AD; historic **cross** in market-place; **tollbridge** on river Ouse.

JUNCTION 36

8½m (13.5km) W on A614, A645 and A1041
Alternative access to **Carlton Towers.** See Junction 34

7m (11km) E to Goole and N on B1228 and A63
Hemingbrough
Typically serene village of Ouse basin; 189ft (58m) spire of lovely 12th-century **church** is a landmark for miles around.

JUNCTION 37

H

1m (1.5km) N on A614
Minster View country hotel, Cornmarket Hill, Howden. Very inexpensive family-type guesthouse, modestly but professionally run; home cooking. Tel: (0430) 30447.

6m (9.5km) NW on A63
Hemingbrough. See Junction 36

JUNCTION 38

8m (13km) NE off B1230

Skidby Windmill Last surviving complete tower windmill in the north, and a big one;

38

B1230
North Cave
Gilberdyke
A63
Hull
Beverley
Humber
Bridge

N

9m(14.4km)

A63
York
A614
Howden
Bridlington

37

3m(4.8km)
to J36

A614
Howden
A63
Selby

---

houses rural museum; milling demonstrations. Close by at Little Weighton, **Rowley Manor** hotel; quiet Georgian house in parkland; 16 rooms; moderately expensive. Tel: (0482) 843132

BEVERLEY

11m (18km) NE on B1230
'A place for walking in and living in,' said poet John Betjeman. The

Minster is considered the purest Gothic example in Europe; **North Bar, North Bar Without** and **North Bar Within** are medieval streets with a few fine Georgian and Regency buildings too; neo-classical **Guildhall** contains ancient civic treasures; older than Minster is **St Nicholas Church,** Newbald; **Museum of Army Transport,** Flemingate, shows tanks, armoured trains, historic staff cars and has 'Cookhouse' tearoom.

13m (21km) NE via Beverley on A1035

Tickton Grange hotel Austere Georgian mansion in charming rural setting; 15 luxurious rooms; five-course dinners, traditional Sun. lunches, roast beef and Yorkshire pudding. Tel: (0401) 43666.

M621:

Birstall to Leeds, 5½m (9km)

There are 3 numbered junctions on this spur from the M62, all giving access to south-west and south-central Leeds. Junction 3, which ends the motorway, continues towards the City Station (BR) as Whitehall Road. It is also Junction 47 on the M1.

JUNCTION 1

3m (5km) W on A6110
Mollie Hillam Porcelain Pottery, Pudsey. One of the more prestigious ceramic workshops and showrooms.

JUNCTION 2

1m (1.5km) W on Kirkstall Road (A65)

Armley Mills A major industrial museum, housed in and around world's largest woollen mill. Diminutive working locomotives are the chief attraction. Closed Mon.

2m (3km) W on Kirkstall Road (A65)

Kirkstall Abbey Awesome perpendicular ruins of monastic building set amid lawns in river glade. **Abbey House,** formerly the gatehouse, is a folk

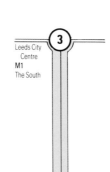

museum incorporating 3 full-sized period streets (gaslamps and cobbles) and typical little shops; slot machines take real old pennies (provided on request). This valley (Aire river and Leeds and Liverpool Canal) carries **Leeds Museum Trail,** 6m (9.5km) long.

JUNCTION 3

1m (1.5km) N to central Leeds
City Art Gallery, Headrow, has splendid impressionist collection plus Henry Moore (born nearby) sculptures.

Leeds City Centre
M1
The South

3

1m(1.6km)

N

Leeds City Centre

2

A643
Beeston

¾m(1.2km)

A6110
Morley
A62

1

A6110
Pudsey
A62

3½m(5.6km)
to M62 (J27)

M63:

Eccles to Stockport, 15m (24km)

Traffic is slowed by perennial roadworks on this arc of motorway which, with the M62 to the north, forms a partial ring route for Manchester; yet there are 12 junctions, spaced out at intervals of about 1m (1.5km), before the route turns into the main road for Sheffield at Junction 13.

Most junctions are linked with major roads from the Liverpool and Chester areas as they converge on central Manchester. The M63 accompanies the river Mersey before the river turns south-west to become a major waterway. Turning east for stockport, the M63 picks up the valley of the Tame. Parts of this valley retain a natural beauty and the plan is to extend them and establish parks and trails.

JUNCTION 2
7m (11km) E on A57
Manchester Access to city, convenient for **Castlefield Urban Heritage Park.** See M602 Junction (3)

JUNCTION 3
7m (11km) E by Redcliffe Road (B5214)
Manchester See M602 Junction (3)

JUNCTION 4
6m (9.6km) E by Parkway (A5081)
Manchester See M602 Junction (3)

JUNCTION 7
4½m (7km) N on A56
Manchester See M602 Junction (3)

7m (11km) S on A56
Dunham Massey Hall, Altrincham. See M56 Junction 7

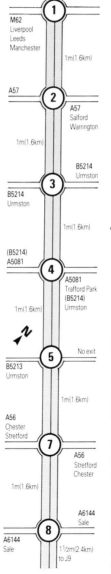

JUNCTION 8

½m (1km) NE on Old Hall Road, signposted at roundabout

Sale and Chorlton Water Parks One of the River Valley Improvement Schemes of Greater Manchester. Sale Park is along the Mersey's south bank, Chorlton Park along the north; bridlepath connects the two; access very near junction, edge of Sale Park; carpark, information office at entrance; each park has its lake; surrounding areas landscaped and planted; gravel footpaths; boating, no swimming; picnic areas; increasing wildlife population, including visiting swans and Canada geese. Open daily in summer, weekends in winter.

133

M63: *11*

JUNCTION 11

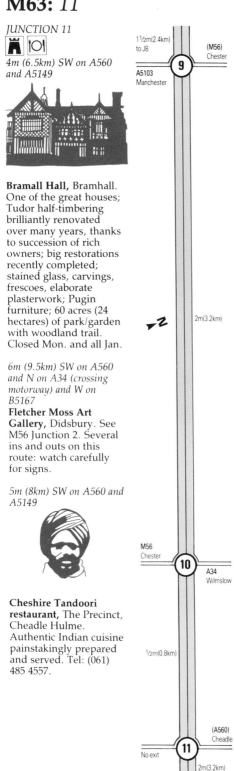

4m (6.5km) SW on A560
and A5149

Bramall Hall, Bramhall.
One of the great houses;
Tudor half-timbering
brilliantly renovated
over many years, thanks
to succession of rich
owners; big restorations
recently completed;
stained glass, carvings,
frescoes, elaborate
plasterwork; Pugin
furniture; 60 acres (24
hectares) of park/garden
with woodland trail.
Closed Mon. and all Jan.

*6m (9.5km) SW on A560
and N on A34 (crossing
motorway) and W on
B5167*
**Fletcher Moss Art
Gallery,** Didsbury. See
M56 Junction 2. Several
ins and outs on this
route: watch carefully
for signs.

*5m (8km) SW on A560 and
A5149*

**Cheshire Tandoori
restaurant,** The Precinct,
Cheadle Hulme.
Authentic Indian cuisine
painstakingly prepared
and served. Tel: (061)
485 4557.

1½m(2.4km)
to J8

(M56)
Chester

9

A5103
Manchester

2m(3.2km)

M56
Chester

10

A34
Wilmslow

½m(0.8km)

(A560)
Cheadle

No exit **11**

2m(3.2km)
to J12

JUNCTION 12

10m (16km) SE on A6

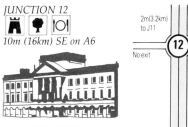

Lyme Park, Disley. Stateliest of Palladian piles (National Trust, formerly Lord Newton); Hall occupies high ground, seems to dominate even Pennines and Derbyshire Peak; Grinling Gibbons carvings; orangery and Dutch garden near house; Park is venue for horse and sheepdog trials; herd of red deer; nature trails, cycle hire (you need a bike to get round the estate); imaginative playground for children; craft shop, cafeteria; not too commercialized, even though the park hosts the Lyme Festival (Aug.). Hall and cafeteria closed in winter.

13m (21km) SE on A6 beyond Disley

Peak Forest Canal, Whaley Bridge. More urbanized than name suggests, the canal pursues a wavering course under dark shoulders of Peak District; towpath walks; narrow boat (capacity 50) with bar and buffet plies N to Marple (7m (11km)).

9m (14.5km) S on A6 and A523
Adlington Hall,

2m(3.2km) to J11

A5145 Didsbury

No exit

12

Adlington. Less frequented than some country houses in Greater Manchester, but good value for architecture; classical portico; Great Hall pillars are 2 ancient oaks; fine organ, said to have been played by Handel. Open Sun. and bank holidays pm only; also certain days in Aug.

JUNCTION 13

5m (8km) NE on A560 and S to Compstall
Etherow Country Park Centre of unspoiled area W, E and S of confluence of Goyt and Etherow rivers; streams, footbridges, old woodlands, many paths; Roman remains; splendid aqueduct and viaduct carry Peak Forest Canal and disused Hayfield Railway; farm trail; interpretative centre in fascinating old sandstone-and-wattle cottage at Chadkirk (footpath from Etherow Park or by Stockport Road, Marple); café and picnic areas; not a chimney or power line in sight.

6m (9.5km) NE on A560 and S to B6101
Sett Valley Trail Low-key but agreeable 2½m (4km) walk from New Mills to Hayfield on track of disused branch railway; also cycle track; route takes in handloom-weaving hamlets, water-powered spinning mills and calico printing factories of long ago; insight into life of secluded, industrious and vanished community.

1½m(2.4km)

A626 Stockport

13

M65:

Blackburn to Colne, 15m (24km)

One day the M65 will be a sinuous route of wide prospects and some natural beauty across the high Pennines and down the Yorkshire dales; a more northerly M62, similarly linking the west-coast and east-coast 'uprights' of Britain's motorway 'ladder'. At present it links only 4 industrial towns of Lancashire: Blackburn, Accrington, Burnley and Nelson. But it runs close to the headwaters of the Aire and Calder rivers, in whose valleys there are pockets of attractive scenery, and it winds among areas of bare moorland of up to 1800ft (549m) which add another dimension to the conventional view of the landscape of Lancashire. The section now open begins at Junction 6 near Blackburn and ends at Junction 13 near Nelson. Only Junctions 10 and 12 are at present fully operational. Junction 8 is intended for a link with the M66 coming north from Manchester.

JUNCTION 6

BLACKBURN
2m (3km) W on A678
Blackburn Museum, Library Street, Preston New Road. Ostensibly a run-of-the-mill municipal museum, but the repository of 1000 delicate and exotic Japanese prints (Hokusai, Utamaro, Hiroshige), bequest of a former cotton-mill magnate; only a few on display, but others will be shown on request; memorabilia of East Lancs Regiment.

4m (6.5km) W on A678 and A674

Witton Country Park, Preston Old Road. Riding and walking trails; schools programmes; visitor centre with agricultural and natural history exhibitions, also arts and crafts shows in summer. Park open daily, visitor centre Thur., Fri., Sat., Sun. and bank holidays only.

A6185
Clitheroe
Accrington

3m(4.8km)
to J8

7

A6185
Clitheroe
Accrington

2¼m(3.6km)

A678
Blackburn
A6119 (A59)
Preston
M6

6

Projected
| | |

JUNCTION 7

½m (1km) N at Clayton-le-Moors on A678

Dunkenhalgh hotel
Park-and-river setting; conferences frequently hosted in the various suites; **Portrait restaurant,** in former drawing-room serves a refined and stylish cuisine; beautiful décor; expensive. Tel: (0254) 398021.

WHALLEY
5m (8km) N on A680
Period-piece village, Tudor and Georgian, attracting many visitors;

Abbey has 2 formidable gateways; 3 **Saxon crosses** in parish churchyard; good picnicking and walking N along Ribble **(Sale Wheel woods)** and S along Calder **(Spring wood).**

136

CLITHEROE

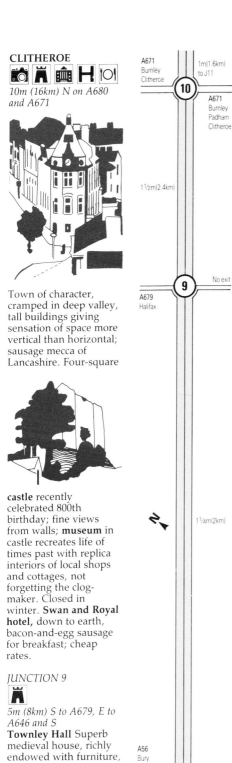

10m (16km) N on A680 and A671

Town of character, cramped in deep valley, tall buildings giving sensation of space more vertical than horizontal; sausage mecca of Lancashire. Four-square

castle recently celebrated 800th birthday; fine views from walls; **museum** in castle recreates life of times past with replica interiors of local shops and cottages, not forgetting the clog-maker. Closed in winter. **Swan and Royal hotel,** down to earth, bacon-and-egg sausage for breakfast; cheap rates.

JUNCTION 9

5m (8km) S to A679, E to A646 and S
Townley Hall Superb medieval house, richly endowed with furniture, paintings, panelling, armour; art gallery has 18th- and 19th-century paintings and summer exhibitions; museum of

crafts and industries (including clogs) in old brewhouse; natural history centre in park.

JUNCTION 10

BURNLEY
1m (1.5km) E to central Burnley

Weavers' Triangle
Atmospheric cluster of early 19th-century cottages at canal wharf; derelict weaving and spinning mills; iron foundry; exhibition at **Canal Toll House,** Manchester Road (Industrial Revolution material, barges); open Sun., Tue. and Wed.; also **boat trips** on Leeds and Liverpool Canal.

PADIHAM
2½m (4km) W on A671
Gawthorpe Hall Mellow high-rise Jacobean mansion with fretted balconies; now a college of education, but Kay-Shuttleworth collection of priceless lace and textiles is visitable; National Trust shop.
Crossways restaurant, Whalley Road; *à la carte* French lunch, dinner; said to be the first French takeaway, call in person or dial-a-meal for pâtés, seafood cocktails, meats and poultry, mouth-watering entremêts; very reasonable prices, but dishes made to order are more expensive. Tel: (0282) 72423.

Map labels

A671
Burnley
Clitheroe

1m(1.6km)
to J11

10

A671
Burnley
Padham
Clitheroe

1½m(2.4km)

9

No exit

A679
Halifax

1¼m(2km)

A56
Bury
Manchester

8

3m(4.8km)
to J7

A56
Accrington
Bury
Manchester

M65: *11-12*

A56
Nelson
Brierfield

12

1m(1.6km)
to J13

A56
Burnley (N)

JUNCTION 11

*2½m (4km) NE off A56,
outskirts of Burnley*

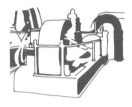

Queen Street Mill
Britain's last steam-
powered cotton mill,
closed 1982 and
reopened as tourist
attraction; exhibition
area, mill shop and café
under development;
open most days, times
have yet to be
standardized.

*3½m (5.5km) SE on
Burnley's 'Greenway'
route*
Hurstwood Charming
small village on Brun
river, shaded with
greenery; among
tottering buildings is
Spenser's Cottage,
reputedly the home of
the Elizabethan poet.

JUNCTION 12

*6m (9.5km) NE on A56, W
on A6068 (recrossing
motorway) and unclassified
road N*
Pendle Hill Steep climb
on narrow road across
shoulder of hill (1831ft
(558m)) of myth and
Gothic horror; stonewall
country, wooded,
pastoral, flowery with
some wildlife; wilder
than any were the

2½m(4km)

Pendle Witches (most of
them hanged at
Lancaster, 1612); see
Harrison Ainsworth's
novel *The Lancashire
Witches* and Robert
Neill's *Mist Over Pendle.*
Hamlets en route are
neat and peaceful,
especially **Newchurch**
and **Barley;** from broad
summit of Pendle
superb views embrace
Blackpool Tower (33m
(53km)) and Lake
District (50m (80km)).

5m (8km) N from Pendle
Downham Serene,
unspoiled village;
stream, village green,
stocks outside archaic
church; considered
Lancashire's prettiest
village.

(A56)
Burnley
Centre

11

No exit

1m(1.6km)
to J10

JUNCTION 13

1m (1.5km) N at junction of A682 and B6247

Pendle Heritage Centre
In 17th-century farmhouse; audio-visual on regional history, notably witchcraft; age-of-elegance gardens under restoration; tearoom. Open pm only, closed Mon., Fri. and all winter.

3m (5km) E on A56
British in India Museum, Sun Street, Colne. Relics of the Raj, mostly photographs, postage-stamps and letters; chief attraction is a working model of the tortuous Kalka-Simla railway. Closed in winter.

6m (9.5km) E on A56 and B6250 via Colne

Wycoller Country Park
All-pedestrian village of Wycoller gives access to large protected area of Trawden Forest; Park opens out from Haworth road; clapper and packhorse bridges on a stream; good walking; best picnic spots for miles around;

A682
Kendal
Skipton
(A6068)
Keighley

Projected

1m(1.6km)
to J12

ruined **Hall** was original of Ferndean Manor in *Jane Eyre.*

12m (19km) E off A6068 at Laneshaw Bridge
Brontë Parsonage, Haworth and **Keighley and Worth Valley Railway.** See M606, Junction (1)

M66:

Edenfield to Manchester, 10m (16km)

At Edenfield, in fine moorland scenery on the skirts of the ancient hunting forest of Rossendale, the A56 going south from Burnley becomes the M66 and follows an undulating route via Bury to the northern suburbs of Manchester. River valleys hereabouts, as in other parts of the Pennines, are dotted with textile mills (some in course of reconstruction as tourist attractions) and with old feudal structures. The first junction is unnumbered; the last is 6m (9.5km) from central Manchester and gives good access to the northern districts of the city.

JUNCTION A

EDENFIELD
½m (1km) NE on A56
One of several attractive villages of the locality.

STUBBINS
1m (1.5km) SW on A676
Stubbins Another attractive village with a waterfall in aptly-named Plunge Valley. The 45m (72km) **Rossendale Way,** a circuit of linked footpaths over moorland with Rossendale (A56) at its centre, passes through Edenfield close to Stubbins.

RAWTENSTALL
8m (13km) N on A56

Ski Rossendale, Haslingden Old Road. England's longest dry-ski slope. **Herbal Health Shop,** Bank Street. Herbalist is heir to a long local tradition.

4m (6.5km) NW on B6214 via A56 and Haslingden bypass
Lancashire Textile Industry Museum, Holcombe Road, Helmshore. Large 3 storeyed early 19th-century mill, formerly steam-powered, demonstrating cotton preparation and spinning; also shuttle

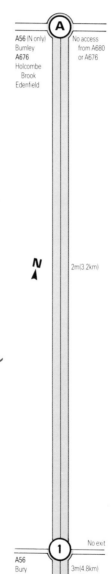

A56 (N only)
Burnley
A676
Holcombe
Brook
Edenfield

No access
from A680
or A676

2m(3.2km)

N ▲

A56
Bury

No exit

3m(4.8km)
to J2

and bobbin manufacture; **Higher Mill Museum** next-door, water-powered, exhibits prototype Hargreaves and Arkwright 'jenny' and water-frame; other historic machines being installed; these 2 buildings intended to be Lancashire's main textiles museum. Closed in winter.

8m (13km) SW on A676

Turton Tower Fierce old pele-tower softened with Victorian 'improvements'; good panelling, wonderfully ornate four-poster bed; own water-wheel and footbridges across railway. Open pm only, closed Mon. and Tue.

JUNCTION 1
9m (14.5km) S and W on Bury bypass and B6196
Turton Tower See previous junction

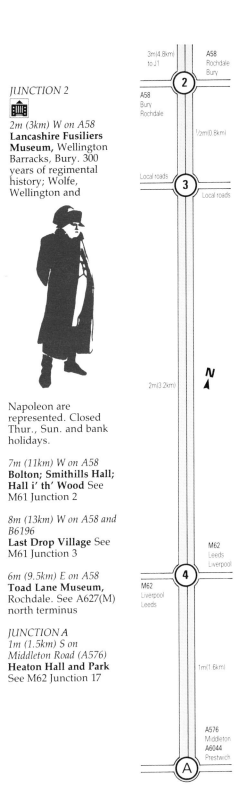

JUNCTION 2

2m (3km) W on A58
Lancashire Fusiliers Museum, Wellington Barracks, Bury. 300 years of regimental history; Wolfe, Wellington and Napoleon are represented. Closed Thur., Sun. and bank holidays.

7m (11km) W on A58
Bolton; Smithills Hall; Hall i' th' Wood See M61 Junction 2

8m (13km) W on A58 and B6196
Last Drop Village See M61 Junction 3

6m (9.5km) E on A58
Toad Lane Museum, Rochdale. See A627(M) north terminus

JUNCTION A
1m (1.5km) S on Middleton Road (A576)
Heaton Hall and Park See M62 Junction 17

M67: Brook

Green to Mottram-in-Longdendale, 6m (9.5km)

You would suppose that this short length of motorway, smoothing a passage into Manchester from the east (Sheffield) side, would be exceptionally busy; but except at commuter times the traffic density is not great. Including the unnumbered terminal junctions (here numbered in brackets) there are 5 junctions. Scenery is urban and suburban. The western end gives access to Manchester's urban ring motorway (M63) and city centre. The eastern end is a launching point for bleak Longdendale and the northern Peak of Derbyshire.

JUNCTION (1)
5m (8km) W on A57
Manchester See M602 terminal junction

JUNCTION 1

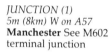

ASHTON-UNDER-LYNE
3m (5km) N on A6017
Parish church has unusually fine stained glass.

Medlock Vale,
edge of town; local 'beauty spot' preserved unspoiled by National Trust.

York House hotel
and restaurant, York Place; 26 rooms; restaurant locally acclaimed for food and wines, but you must dine before 9.30 pm. Tel: (061) 330 5899.

JUNCTION 2

DUKINFIELD
2m (3km) N on B6170
Self-contained community not swamped by suburbia.

Newton Hall, S on Dukinfield Road; charming timbered manor-farmhouse. Adjacent, along **Tame Valley** and **Peak Forest Canal,** dredging and face-lifting of waterways in progress; footpaths and towpaths facilitate access to picturesque old cottages and industrial-archaeological relics, notably bridges; walks extend S to Stockport (11m (17.5km)) and N to Denshaw beyond Oldham (13m (22km)); towpath of **Huddersfield Narrow Canal** where verges are tidied and locks cascaded is particularly interesting between Portland Basin (Ashton-under-Lyne bypass) and Uppermill (near Oldham); but rough going in places — the improvement scheme is a long-term project.

A57
Denton
Manchester

¾am(1.2km)

No exit

¾am(1.2km)
to J3

1

A6017
Ashton
Stockport

JUNCTION 3
2½m (4km) N on B6175
Alternative access to
Dukinfield and **Tame
Valley.** See Junction 2

*4m (6.5km) S via Hyde, off
A560*
Etherow Country Park,
Compstall. See M63
Junction 13

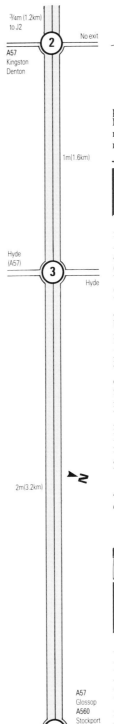

3/4m (1.2km)
to J2

(2) No exit

A57
Kingston
Denton

1m(1.6km)

Hyde
(A57)

(3)

Hyde

2m(3.2km)

⊿N

A57
Glossop
A560
Stockport

(4)

point for **Peak District
National Park,** grouse-
moors, desolate but
romantic (for highest

moor, **Kinderscout,** take
A57 E from junction and
at 4m (7km) walk 2m
(3km) S on **Pennine
Way**); 7m (12km) NE of
Glossop the Pennine
Way again crosses A628
and B6105 at **Crowden;**
boating, sailing
instruction at **Torside
Reservoir;** at E end of
riverine lake **Woodhead
Tunnel** (3m (5km) long)
on disused Manchester-
Sheffield-Lincoln
railway. **Wind in the
Willows hotel** and
restaurant, Sheffield
Road; 7 well-appointed
rooms; genuine homely
atmosphere; expensive.
Tel: (045 74) 3354.

*4m (6.5km) E on A57,
entering Glossop*

Dinting Railway Centre
Historic locomotives
assembled in former
Great Central Steam
Depot; steam raised and
free rides offered on
summer Sundays;
miniature railway;
souvenir shop,
refreshment room,
picnic area.

JUNCTION (4)

📷 ❀ **H** 🍴 🏛

GLOSSOP
5½m (9km) E on A57
Small town known to
the Romans; later
known to visitors as
smoky and inhospitable;
now bright, tourist-
orientated and an access

M69:

Ansty to Leicester Forest, 16m (26km)

This route is a link between the M6 in Warwickshire and the M1 in Leicestershire and between the 2 cities of Coventry and Leicester; and, to judge by the traffic density on weekdays, many motorists and heavy goods vehicle drivers find it useful. Being very much an A-to-B kind of route, it has not much to offer the wide-ranging tourist; and the low-lying East Midlands agricultural country through which its course is driven has few distinguishing features. There are 2 intermediate junctions in the middle section of the route, fairly close together.

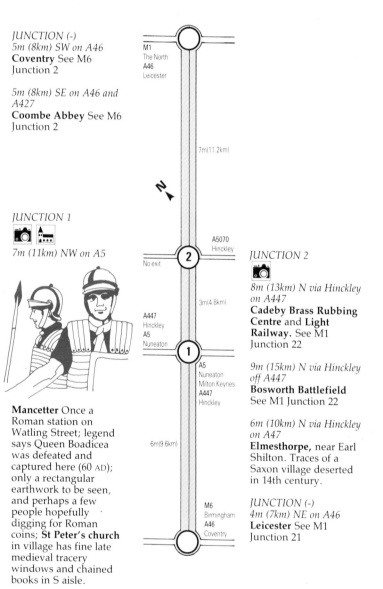

JUNCTION (-)
5m (8km) SW on A46
Coventry See M6 Junction 2

5m (8km) SE on A46 and A427
Coombe Abbey See M6 Junction 2

JUNCTION 1

7m (11km) NW on A5

Mancetter Once a Roman station on Watling Street; legend says Queen Boadicea was defeated and captured here (60 AD); only a rectangular earthwork to be seen, and perhaps a few people hopefully digging for Roman coins; **St Peter's church** in village has fine late medieval tracery windows and chained books in S aisle.

M1
The North
A46
Leicester

7m(11.2km)

A5070
Hinckley

2

No exit

3m(4.8km)

A447
Hinckley
A5
Nuneaton

1

A5
Nuneaton
Milton Keynes
A447
Hinckley

6m(9.6km)

M6
Birmingham
A46
Coventry

JUNCTION 2

8m (13km) N via Hinckley on A447
Cadeby Brass Rubbing Centre and **Light Railway.** See M1 Junction 22

9m (15km) N via Hinckley off A447
Bosworth Battlefield See M1 Junction 22

6m (10km) N via Hinckley on A47
Elmesthorpe, near Earl Shilton. Traces of a Saxon village deserted in 14th century.

JUNCTION (-)
4m (7km) NE on A46
Leicester See M1 Junction 21

A627 (M):

Oldham to Rochdale, 4m (6.5km)

A short urban route which crosses
the M62. One intermediate junction
is the interchange with that
motorway, the other — by way of a
1m (1.5km) spur — provides access
to the A664 Manchester-Rochdale
road. These junctions, as well as the
2 termini, are unnumbered (here
numbered in brackets).

*JUNCTION (1) (terminus
at Oldham)*

📷 🏛 🍽

*5m (8km) E on A669 and
A670.*

Alexandra Craft Centre,
Uppermill, near
Saddleworth. Former
woollen mill, now a
busy commercial crafts
and souvenir enterprise;
has been featured on
TV; tearooms; opposite,

the **Saddleworth
Museum,** chiefly
Victoriana; carpark at
museum. **Moorcock
restaurant,** The Hey,
Saddleworth. Tel: (045
77) 2659. Good value,
no-nonsense fare on a
steepish climb to the
moors.

*JUNCTION (2) (spur to
A664)*
*4½m (7km) SW on A664
and A576*
Heaton Park See M62
Junction 17

*2½m (4km) S off A664 at
Cheetham Hill*
**Manchester Museum of
Transport** See M62
Junction 19

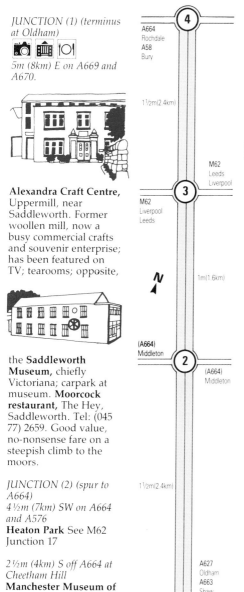

*JUNCTION (4) (terminus
at Rochdale)*

🏛

1½m (2km) N on A58

Toad Lane Museum, off
St Mary's Gate,
Rochdale. Shop opened
by 'Rochdale Pioneers'
in 1844; now elaborated
and enlarged as the
museum of the co-
operative movement
worldwide.

M73:

Uddingston to Mollinsburn, 6½m (10km)

This short link from the M74 and the A80/M80 will one day be a section of a motorway from Carlisle to the central Highlands of Scotland. It speeds the motorist across the least pleasant part of that route: the eastern suburbs of Glasgow, a scene of confusing roads and streets, acres of housing estates and a notorious deprivation in districts such as Easterhouse.

JUNCTION 1

🌳 🏰 📷 🏛️

¾m (1km) W on Hamilton Road

Calderpark Zoo The Glasgow zoological gardens, long-established, small, visited mainly by locals; undergoing long-term development, an ambitious open plan; cats and reptiles are special features; picnic area, children's playground.

5m (8km) S on B7078.

Bothwell Castle and **Bothwell Brig** Once the biggest castle in Scotland, now a ruin; Brig (bridge) on Clyde river was scene of crucial battle when Monmouth and Claverhouse destroyed Covenanters' armies, 1679 (for an account, see Scott's *Old Mortality*); parts of old brig incorporated in modern bridge, which is a busy traffic interchange.

7½m (12km) S on B7012 via Bothwell

David Livingstone

A80 (N only) — Access from A80(S) only

5m(8km)

M8 Glasgow
A8 Edinburgh (M8)
Glasgow

A8 Glasgow (Centre) Edinburgh (M8)

2m(3.2km)

M74 The South Carlisle Glasgow (SE)

Memorial Splendid complex of buildings and gardens built round the missionary-explorer's humble birthplace on Clyde bank, off Station Road, Blantyre; well signposted; a major Scottish museum-centre with tearoom, library and lecture hall; attracts African students.

JUNCTION 3

KIRKINTILLOCH
5m (8km) NW on A80 and B757
Quiet, straggling village with distinction of being on both 200-year-old

Forth and Clyde canal (towpath walks, boat excursions from Stables Inn) and 1800-year-old **Antonine Wall,** the Scottish equivalent of Hadrian's Wall; few traces of wall survive, but two of the most important fragments are visible at Cadder (3m (5km) W) and Bar Hill (3m (5km) E).

146

M74:
Blackwood to Uddingston, 12½m (20km)

When the M74, Glasgow-Carlisle, is completed it will be among Britain's most beautiful motorways, especially on the southern sections where it will climb through the Tinto and Lowther hills and descend with sweeping bends and wide vistas down the valley of the infant Clyde. The section now open begins in the middle Clyde valley and makes its way into a somewhat decayed industrial landscape, where the river of Glasgow runs alongside, no longer the innocent stream of pebbly shallows, rushing rapids and salmon leaps that old writers enthused over.

At its northern end the M74 merges with the M73 to form a sort of Glasgow bypass and a useful fast route between the Border country and the central Highlands. At the southern end there are several junctions under construction (unnumbered); the first numbered junction is 2.

JUNCTION (-)

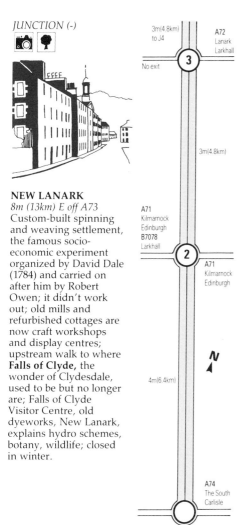

NEW LANARK
8m (13km) E off A73
Custom-built spinning and weaving settlement, the famous socio-economic experiment organized by David Dale (1784) and carried on after him by Robert Owen; it didn't work out; old mills and refurbished cottages are now craft workshops and display centres; upstream walk to where **Falls of Clyde,** the wonder of Clydesdale, used to be but no longer are; Falls of Clyde Visitor Centre, old dyeworks, New Lanark, explains hydro schemes, botany, wildlife; closed in winter.

(map:)
3m(4.8km) to J4
No exit
3 A72 Lanark Larkhall
3m(4.8km)

A71 Kilmarnock Edinburgh B7078 Larkhall
2 A71 Kilmarnock Edinburgh

N

4m(6.4km)

A74 The South Carlisle

JUNCTION 2

STRATHAVEN
5m (8km) SW on A71 (pronounced 'Straiven')
Dull-looking village with unexpectedly interesting features; **John Hastie Museum** of local history, Strathaven

Park; **Avondale Castle,** 15th-century ruin romantically sited above Avon river; **theatre-and-arts centre** in well-preserved 17th-century grain mill and granary; **Lauder Ha',** just outside village, mini-stately home built by Harry Lauder in days of his comic-song renown.

M74: 4-6

JUNCTION 4

🏛️ 🌳 📷 🏘️

1½m (2.5km) W off A723

Cameronians Regimental Museum, Muir Street, Hamilton. Historical material dating back to 'killing times' of Covenanting memory during religious wars of late 1660s and 1670s.

1m (1.5km) W off A723
Strathclyde Country Park Stretches along both sides of motorway, near confluence of Avon and Clyde; last bit of green countryside that Glasgow-bound motorists will see for a while; contains

grandiose **Hamilton Mausoleum** (huge bronze doors, amazing echo inside) where Dukes of Hamilton are buried.

4m (6.5km) E off A723 via Motherwell
Carfin Grotto Most important shrine in Scotland, dedicated to Our Lady of Lourdes and incorporating stones from Lourdes; smaller shrines adorn the gardens; tearoom

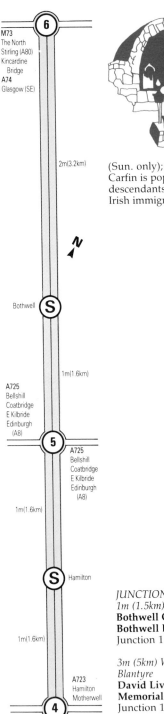

(Sun. only); village of Carfin is populated by descendants of Catholic Irish immigrants.

---

⑥

M73
The North
Stirling (A80)
Kincardine
Bridge
A74
Glasgow (SE)

2m (3.2km)

Ⓢ Bothwell

1m(1.6km)

A725
Bellshill
Coatbridge
E Kilbride
Edinburgh
(A8)

⑤

A725
Bellshill
Coatbridge
E Kilbride
Edinburgh
(A8)

1m(1.6km)

Ⓢ Hamilton

1m(1.6km)

A723
Hamilton
Motherwell

④

A723
Hamilton
Motherwell

3m(4.8km)
to J3

JUNCTION 5
1m (1.5km) W on A725
Bothwell Castle and **Bothwell Brig** See M73 Junction 1

3m (5km) W on A725 at Blantyre
David Livingstone Memorial See M73 Junction 1

JUNCTION 6
¾m (1km) W on Hamilton Road
Calderpark Zoo See M73 Junction 1

M8: Newbridge to Langbank, 50m (80km); incorporates M77 (Pollok spur, 1m (1.5km)) and M898 (Erskine Bridge spur, 1m (1.5km)).

Scotland's longest motorway runs from sea to sea, from the Firth of Forth in the east to the Firth of Clyde in the west. Its first junction, numbered 2, is within easy reach of Edinburgh's suburbs. Like the first Roman wall and the first Scottish ship canal before highways came to Scotland, the motorway then travels across the country's wasp waist, the mining and industrial central belt. It ends temporarily at Junction 6 and begins again at Junction 8.

Between Junctions 8 and 30 the M8 skims across the great city of Glasgow and its satellite towns, where half the population of Scotland is concentrated. It rides above the tenements, glimpses city landmarks and distant hills from panoramic angles and gives a perspective of the city which Glaswegians themselves never knew until the motorway came. On this section of about 18 miles (29km) there are no fewer than 22 junctions (we group them below under the general heading of Glasgow).

The end of the M8 comes just as the Clyde begins to broaden towards its firth, exchanging the gaunt Clydeside shipyards for the green mountains of Argyll to the north and the woods and dunes of Ayrshire's celebrated 'golf coast' to the west and south.

JUNCTION 2

📷 H 🍴

3½m (5.5km) E on A8
Suntrap An agricultural college garden, propagating and advice centre, especially designed for the edification of the small-time gardener.

4m (6.5km) N on A8000 via M9 link

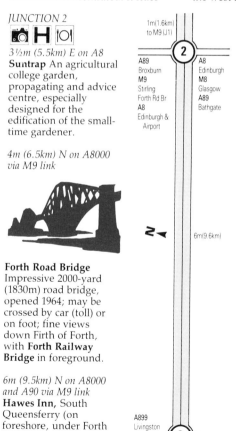

Forth Road Bridge
Impressive 2000-yard (1830m) road bridge, opened 1964; may be crossed by car (toll) or on foot; fine views down Firth of Forth, with **Forth Railway Bridge** in foreground.

6m (9.5km) N on A8000 and A90 via M9 link
Hawes Inn, South Queensferry (on foreshore, under Forth Railway Bridge). Historic black-and-white many-gabled ferry inn, scene of incidents in R.L. Stevenson's

Kidnapped; 7 atmospheric rooms; restaurant offers elaborate cuisine at prices expensive by Scottish country standards; can be crowded at weekends. Tel: Edinburgh 331 1990.

JUNCTION 3

🌳 🍴 📷

6m (9.5km) E off minor roads from Livingston or Broxburn
Almondell Country Park Laid out by international organization called *Enterprise Youth*; paths and footbridges along Almond river; visitor centre.

3m (5km) SW via Livingston off A705
Livingston Mill Farm, Kirkton. Reconstructed 18th-century farm-steading; water-mill, animal paddock, picnic area; light meals in farm kitchen; all low-key and informal. Open Sat., Sun. or by appointment; closed winter weekdays.

Diagram labels:

1m(1.6km) to M9 (J1)

2

A89 Broxburn M9 Stirling Forth Rd Br A8 Edinburgh & Airport

A8 Edinburgh M8 Glasgow A89 Bathgate

N ←

6m(9.6km)

A899 Livingston

3

A899 Livingston

6m(9.6km) to J4

M8: 4-26

JUNCTION 4

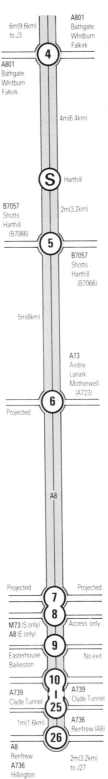

5m (8km) N on B792
Cairnpapple Hill,
Torphichen. Former
neolithic temple and
Bronze Age burial site;
excavations and
reconstructions
traceable; close by,
Torphichen Priory,
former HQ of Knights
Hospitallers in Scotland,
whose history from
medieval times is
portrayed in the small
fortress-like (16th-
century) church.

JUNCTION 6

*4½m (7km) SW on
A721/A723*
Carfin Grotto See M74
Junction 4

**(Motorway ends and
begins again at
Junction 8)**

JUNCTION 8

2m (3km) S on M73
Calderpark Zoo See
M73 Junction 1

JUNCTIONS 9 to 26

GLASGOW
N and S
All junctions, which are
closely spaced, lead into
the Glasgow
conurbation; E junctions
convenient for
Glasgow's ancient
heart, **St Mungo's**

**Cathedral, Provan's
Lordship** and other
historic monuments
(which are few); middle
junctions serve the
modern city centre,
imposing **City
Chambers,** theatres,
cinemas, restaurants
and principal hotels; W
junctions are gateways
to Glasgow of much-
admired Victorian
terraces and crescents
and of beautiful
parkland including

Kelvingrove Park and
Botanical Gardens (N of
Clyde), famous **Art
Gallery** (N of Clyde),
Pollok Park with
notable country-house
museums and modern
(1982) custom-built
Burrell Gallery housing
large and controversial
Burrell Collection (S of
Clyde); from Junction 22
the M77 spur (1m
(1.5km)) leads S towards
Kilmarnock.

Central motorway diagram

A801
Bathgate
Whitburn
Falkirk

6m(9.6km)
to J3

4

A801
Bathgate
Whitburn
Falkirk

4m(6.4km)

S Harthill

B7057
Shotts
Harthill
(B7066)

2m(3.2km)

5

B7057
Shotts
Harthill
(B7066)

5m(8km)

A73
Airdrie
Lanark
Motherwell
(A723)

6

Projected

A8

Projected   Projected

7
8

M73 (S only)   Access only
A8 (E only)

9

Easterhouse   No exit
Baillieston

10
I
25

A739   A739
Clyde Tunnel   Clyde Tunnel

1m(1.6km)   A736
                     Renfrew (A8)

26

A8
Renfrew   2m(3.2km)
A736   to J27
Hillington

150

JUNCTION 27

1m (1.5km) S on Renfrew Road

Paisley Abbey 12th-century abbey, much restored; contains tombs of Scottish royalty including Marjory Bruce, mother of the Stuart dynasty; close by, in Paisley High Street,

Paisley Museum houses principal collection of Paisley shawls and silkwear and shows history of locally-invented 'Paisley' weaving pattern.

JUNCTION 28

½m (1km) N on airport road

Excelsior hotel and **restaurant** Adjacent to main Glasgow airport building; one of Glasgow's superior and luxurious establishments, possibly the best airport hotel in Britain; not outrageously expensive. Tel: Glasgow 887 1212.

JUNCTION 29
2m (3km) E on A726
Paisley Abbey See Junction 27

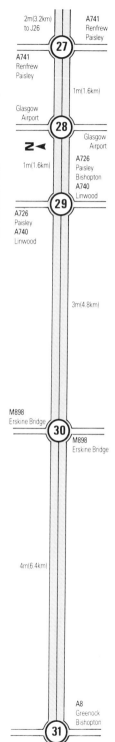

2m(3.2km) to J26

A741 Renfrew Paisley

27

A741 Renfrew Paisley

1m(1.6km)

Glasgow Airport

28

Glasgow Airport

1m(1.6km)

A726 Paisley Bishopton
A740 Linwood

29

A726 Paisley
A740 Linwood

3m(4.8km)

M898 Erskine Bridge

30

M898 Erskine Bridge

4m(6.4km)

A8 Greenock Bishopton

31

JUNCTION 30

Junction with M898, a short spur to **Erskine** (road) **Bridge** on the Clyde.

1½m (2km) N via M898 and B815

Blantyre Monument Tall obelisk commemorating Lord Blantyre, killed in Brussels riots, 1830; the former Blantyre seat, **Erskine House,** now a hospital for war-disabled, stands nearby.

JUNCTION 31

1m (1.5km) NW on B789

Gleddoch House hotel, Langbank. Country-house elegance and *cordon bleu* cuisine; fine situation, magnificent views across Clyde; fairly expensive. Tel: (047 554) 771.

2m (3km) W on A8
Finlaystone House with Robert Burns and John Knox associations; big collection of dolls of all nations; gardens, woodland walks, adventure playground. House open Apr.-Aug., Sun. or by appointment.

6m (9.5km) W on A8

Newark Castle Handsome turreted mansion, partly 15th-century, sparsely furnished; worth visiting for splendid seascapes from upper floors.

M80:

Dennyloanhead to Bannockburn, 5m (8km)

The M80 is a short linking route, forming a small triangle of motorways where, one day, motorways from Carlisle and Glasgow to Stirling (M74 and M73) and from Edinburgh to Stirling (M9) will come together. The first junction is numbered 4, the single intermediate junction (5) is close by, and the route merges with the M9 at Junction 9.

JUNCTION 4

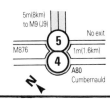

1½m (2.5km) S on A80/B816
Rough Castle Grass-grown ramparts and ditches marking a station on **Antonine Wall** (142 AD); best-preserved of forts on Roman Great Wall.

```
            5m(8km)
            to M9 (J9)
                        No exit
                   (5)
M876               |  1m(1.6km)
                   (4)
                     A80
            N        Cumbernauld
```

M85:

Craigend to Kinfauns, 1½m (2.5km)

So short as to be little more than a river bridge, the M85 strikes north from the M90, leaps across the Tay and lands on the Perth-Dundee road (A85). It opens up spectacular views of Perth to the west, and to the broadening Firth of Tay to the east. Its terminus (where the one-way system gives no access to Perth) is numbered Junction 1.

JUNCTION 1

1m (1.5km) W by footpath off A85 (vehicles travel E and make U-turn at first main road junction)
Kinnoull Hill Superb views from this 729ft (223m) summit; Fife, Tay and Grampian highlands visible.

1m (1.5km) W on A85 (U-turn as in preceding entry)

Branklyn Garden
National Trust; under Kinnoull Hill; described as 'finest two acres of garden in Scotland'; experimentation centre for exotic shrubs and plants; remarkable for meconopsis, rhododendrons, hydrangeas and conifers.

```
            (1)
A85
The N East
Dundee
Forfar
Aberdeen
A93
Perth
Braemar

     N

1½m(2.4km)

M90
The North &
West
Stirling (A9)
Inverness
(A9)
M90
The South
Forth Rd Br
Kincardine
Bridge
            (10)
Access from
M90
```

PERTH
1½m (2.5km) W on A85 (U-turn as in preceding entries)

Excellent **shopping centre; Fair Maid's House,** North Port, a good crafts centre; **Round House,** former fire brigade HQ of interesting design, now tourist centre with audio-visual travelogues; **Black Watch regimental museum,** Hay Street, closed Sat. in summer, Sat. and Sun. in winter; **Coach House restaurant,** North Port (opposite Fair Maid's House) has period layout and extensive and imaginative *à la carte*; attracts many tourists in summer. Tel: (0738) 27950.

M876:

Dennyloanhead to Stenhousemuir, 7m (11km)

Like the M80, the M876 is one leg of the motorway triangle at the nexus of Edinburgh, Stirling and Glasgow routes. Its function will be more apparent at some distant date in the future, when a motorway across the upper Forth connects Glasgow with Perth, Dundee and Aberdeen. There are 6 junctions, only 3 of them numbered. Like all the motorways in this region of Scotland, traffic is light by English standards.

JUNCTION 1
3m (5km) S on B816
Rough Castle See M80 Junction 4

JUNCTION 2

4m (6.5km) E on A9

Scottish Railway Preservation Society, Wallace Street, Falkirk. In the depressing surroundings of an old railway freight yard, a few historic locomotives and some miscellaneous rolling stock are undergoing restoration; plenty of nostalgia for rail buffs; small shop; open Sat. and Sun. only; connected with the Bo'ness and Kinneil Railway (see M9 Junction 3).

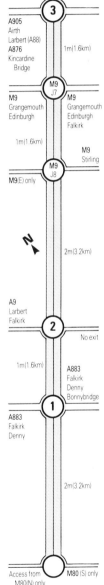

③
A905 Airth Larbert (A88) A876 Kincardine Bridge — 1m(1.6km)

M9 J7 — M9 Grangemouth Edinburgh / M9 Grangemouth Edinburgh Falkirk

1m(1.6km) — M9 Stirling

M9 J8 — M9(E) only

2m(3.2km)

A9 Larbert Falkirk

② — No exit

1m(1.6km) — A883 Falkirk Denny Bonnybridge

①

A883 Falkirk Denny

2m(3.2km)

Access from M80(N) only — M80 (S) only

JUNCTION 3

1½m (2.5km) NW on A905
Airth Castle hotel and restaurant. 14th-century building extensively modernized and flourishing as an expensive country-house hotel; sophisticated and cosmopolitan cuisine, mainly French flavour. Tel: (032 483) 411.

4m (7km) NW via Airth on B9124

Dunmore Pineapple Dated 1791, this stone pineapple is the centrepiece of **Dunmore Park's** formal gardens; available as holiday cottage through Landmark Trust or National Trust for Scotland.

6m (9.5km) NE on A985 via Kincardine Bridge
Culross (pronounced 'Cooruss'). Intact 16th/17th-century coastal village with diminutive palace, town hall, abbey, numerous crow-stepped and pantiled cottages on narrow lanes.

M9:
Kirkliston to Dunblane, 32m (51km)

The M9 might be called the Royal Route, since it begins near the capital city, Edinburgh, and ends near the old Scottish capital, Stirling; and along the way has a fine close-up view of Linlithgow Palace, another spot renowned in the history of the Stuart kings and queens. The route follows the south shore of the Firth of Forth, but offers only occasional glimpses of that waterway; mostly it rides across pleasant agricultural country and parkland, which is interrupted only by its crossing of the rough industrial belt near Falkirk. The BP oil refinery at Grangemouth and the Carron Iron Works (which supplied cannon to Nelson's navy, hence 'carronade') are among the landmarks of this section.

At its eastern end, the M9 is linked with the beginning of the M8 motorway; at its western, it comes to an end where the appetizing country of the Ochil hills and Perthshire highlands rise from the landscape. One of the quietest motorways in Britain.

JUNCTION 1
3m (5km) N on A8000
Forth Road Bridge See M8 Junction 2

4½m (7km) N on A8000 and A90
Hawes Inn, South Queensferry. See M8 Junction 2

JUNCTION 2

2½m (4km) N off A904
Hopetoun House Vast, rather soulless-looking Adam mansion (Marquess of Linlithgow); rich furnishings, valuable family portraits including a Rembrandt; enormous deer park slopes to Forth shore;

Scottish Horse Museum in stable block. Closed in winter.

3m (5km) N off A904
House of the Binns Four-square castellated mansion dating back 350 years to General Tam Dalyell who fought in

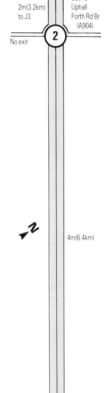

2m(3.2km) to J3

No exit

B8046
Uphall
Forth Rd Br
(A904)

2

4m(6.4km)

(A8000)
Forth Rd Br

1

No exit

1m(1.6km) to M8 (J2)

Civil and Covenanting wars; excellent example of old-style fortified dwelling progressively refined and made comfortable; visitor trail in hilly park offers good views of lands beyond the Forth. Closed Fri. and all winter.

3m (5km) N on B903

Blackness Castle Pugnacious seafront fort, unimproved since 15th century, with ram bow pushing into Forth like a battleship; has been state prison, powder magazine and youth hostel but present role, to be quite deserted, suits it best; unique views of upper and lower Forth. Closed Mon. and Tue. in winter.

JUNCTION 3

2½m (4km) W on A803

Linlithgow Palace Set in heart of town, like so many old Scottish palaces, and linked to main street by gatehouse, portcullis and bridge on a one-time moat; 16th-century decorated stone fountain in quadrangle, a twin of that at Holyrood Palace, Edinburgh; Great Hall, scene of events in Scottish history; bedchamber where Mary Queen of Scots was born in 1542.

4½m (7km) N on A904
Bo'ness and Kinneil Railway, Bo'ness station, Union Street, Bo'ness. On summer weekends, Edwardian-style booking clerk at period-piece booking office sells tickets for short trip on restored track; steam locomotives; rolling stock collection on view; Buffer Stop café; visitor trail along the route, which is gradually being extended towards Linlithgow. Open weekends only.

JUNCTION 4
3m (5km) SE on A803
Linlithgow Palace See Junction 3

JUNCTION 5

2m (3km) N on A905/A904
'Paraffin' Young Exhibition, BP

Information Centre, Grangemouth. Traces progress of petro-chemicals industry from 19th-century experiments of James 'Paraffin' Young, chemist who first demonstrated commercial potential of shale-oil products. Closed Sat:, Sun. and all winter.

JUNCTION 6
2½m (4km) N on A905
'Paraffin' Young Exhibition See Junction 5

2½m (4km) SW on A904
Scottish Railway Preservation Society See M876 Junction 2

JUNCTION 9

1½m (2½km) N on A9
Bannockburn Lavish celebration in concrete and metal of battle of 1314, date which Scots associate above all others with national pride and self-determination; equestrian statue of

Robert the Bruce on hilltop; large hall at roadside incorporates cinema, lecture theatre, shops, information centre and National Trust shop; large impressive mural depicts battle; audio-visual presentations. (Actual site of battle is now thought to have been on lower ground, some distance E.)

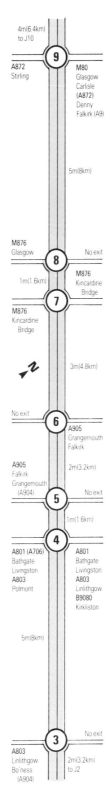

4m(6.4km) to J10

9

A872 Stirling

M80 Glasgow Carlisle (A872) Denny Falkirk (A9)

5m(8km)

M876 Glasgow

8 No exit

M876 Kincardine Bridge

1m(1.6km)

7

M876 Kincardine Bridge

3m(4.8km)

No exit **6**

A905 Grangemouth Falkirk

A905 Falkirk Grangemouth (A904)

2m(3.2km)

5 No exit

1m(1.6km)

4

A801 (A706) Bathgate Livingston A803 Polmont

A801 Bathgate Livingston A803 Linlithgow B9080 Kirkliston

5m(8km)

3 No exit

A803 Linlithgow Bo'ness (A904)

2m(3.2km) to J2

M9: *10-11*

JUNCTION 10

STIRLING
1m (1.5km) E on A84

Noted for great royal
castle on rocky bluff, a
powerful military
fortress for 7 centuries;
contains expensively-
restored Great Hall and
regimental museum of
Argyll and Sutherland
Highlanders; splendid
views from ramparts, W
towards Ben Lomond
and Ben Ledi; on steep
descent to town, old
crow-stepped buildings
of former Stuart
courtiers; **Old Brig** on
River Forth near town
centre figured
prominently in Scottish
history.

6m (9.5km) W on A84

**Blair Drummond Safari
Park** First in Scotland,
with lions, tigers,
camels, giraffes and
mischievous monkeys
with a passion for
windscreen wipers; boat
trips on small lake
follow trail of chimps
and hippos; sealion
show; many fairground
amusements.

11

B824 (A820)
Doune
A9
Perth
Bridge of
Allan

N

3m(4.8km)

A84 (A9)
Stirling

10

A84 (A85)
Callander
Crianlarich
Stirling

4m(6.4km)
to J9

JUNCTION 11

4m (6.5km) W on B824

**Doune Castle and
Motor Museum**
Imposing medieval ruin
(Earl of Moray)
mentioned in old ballad
The Bonnie Earl o'Moray;
vintage and classic
motor-car collection in
castle grounds,
emphasis on heavy
British and Continental
marques. Closed in
winter.

1m (1.5km) N on A9

Dunblane Cathedral
Here, in what is now a
pleasant commuter
town, St Blane settled in
6th century; cathedral,
mainly 12th-century,
lost its roof at
Reformation;
painstakingly restored
in Victoria's reign,
building was
particularly admired by
John Ruskin, arbiter of
Gothic taste; charming
old **Dean's House,**
Cathedral Square,
houses museum and
library.

3½m (5.5km) N on B8033
Cromlix House hotel,
Kinbuck. Hoary old
fortified house, noted
for gracious living; 11
rooms, usually full, but
restaurant serves
memorable dishes,
especially soups and
seafoods; expensive.
Tel: (0786) 822125.

M90:

Forth Bridge to Perth, 31m (49km)

The M90, the only entirely rural motorway in Scotland, connects the Firth of Forth with Firth of Tay, skirting en route the 'kingdom' of Fife. Much of the journey is open and breezy and traffic is sometimes affected by crosswinds. The scenery consists mainly of undulating landscapes with panoramas of loch and hill (Loch Leven and the Lomond hills — nothing to do with Loch Lomond) which offer a foretaste of the Highland country towards which the motorway is leading. On a clear day, as it descends towards Perth from the last complicated interchange, there are splendid views of the Tay estuary, the Augus hills and the outspread city of Perth — views which caused 19th-century travellers to call this district the 'Scottish Rhineland'.

JUNCTION 1

4m (6.5km) S on A90
Forth Road Bridge See M8 Junction 2

ABERDOUR
5m (8km) E on A921
Pretty little seaside resort with minuscule beach, harbour and 14th-century **castle** (closed Fri.) standing guard; 10-minute boat trip, frequent services in summer, to **Inchcolm,** holy island of Firth of

Forth, with small **abbey** which, though a ruin, escaped actual destruction at Reformation and is therefore among Scotland's best-preserved medieval ecclesiastical monuments.

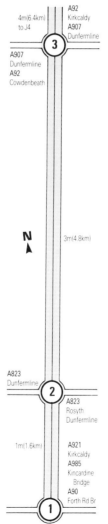

[map, from bottom to top:]

1 — A921 Kirkcaldy / A985 Kincardine Bridge / A90 Forth Rd Br
1m(1.6km)
A823 Dunfermline — **2** — A823 Rosyth Dunfermline
3m(4.8km)
N ▲
A907 Dunfermline / A92 Cowdenbeath — **3** — A92 Kirkcaldy / A907 Dunfermline
4m(6.4km) to J4

JUNCTION 2

DUNFERMLINE
3m (5km) W on A823
'The King sits in Dunfermline toun/Drinking the blude-red wine' — it was a seat of kings and is now a busy town on precipitous streets; confusing traffic pattern; on Monastery Street, great **abbey church** where Robert the Bruce was buried and King Charles I was born; in Moodie Street, humble birthplace of plutocrat-philanthropist Andrew Carnegie, a Mecca for American tourists (in winter, pm only); on W side of town, lavishly-endowed **Pittencrieff Park** and **Glen,** with ravines, floral

extravaganzas, peacocks and miniature train — a Carnegie bequest.

8m (13km) W on A985
Culross See M876 Junction 3

JUNCTION 3
3m (5km) W on A907
Dunfermline See Junction 2

M90: 4-7

JUNCTION 4

4m (6.5km) E on B920

Lochore Meadows Large country park reclaimed from wastelands of old Fife coalfield; watersports and fishing on artificial lake; wayfaring; resident ranger offers guided walks and botany lessons; café, picnic areas; a developing site.

JUNCTION 5

8m (13km) W on B9097
Rumbling Bridge Deep romantic chasm; where steep footpath from Rumbling Bridge hotel comes to water's edge, the River Devon burbles impressively after heavy rain; 1m (1½km) downstream, another thunderous canyon called **Cauldron Linn.**

3m (5km) E off B9097
Vane Farm Agricultural buildings converted to an interpretative display centre for surrounding countryside; hill paths radiate from it; on nearby Loch Leven shore, observation points for wildfowl (binoculars provided).

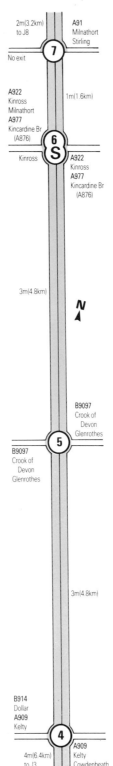

2m(3.2km) to J8

A91 Milnathort Stirling

No exit

7

1m(1.6km)

A922 Kinross Milnathort
A977 Kincardine Br (A876)

Kinross

6 S

A922 Kinross
A977 Kincardine Br (A876)

3m(4.8km)

N

B9097 Crook of Devon Glenrothes

5

B9097 Crook of Devon Glenrothes

3m(4.8km)

B914 Dollar
A909 Kelty

4

A909 Kelty Cowdenbeath

4m(6.4km) to J3

JUNCTION 6

1m (1.5km) E on A922

Kinross Quiet small town, though once a county centre; doorsteps lapped by Loch Leven, whose distinctive pink-bellied trout are usually visible; many marshfowl and waterfowl; mid-loch island (boat excursions in summer) has a ruined castle from which Mary Queen of Scots escaped after a year's imprisonment in 1568. **Green hotel,** High Street; once an important coaching inn and traditionally a well-conducted, not expensive, establishment; indoor curling rink; restaurant and bar meals, venison and Tay salmon. Tel: (0577) 63467.

JUNCTION 7

1m (1.5km) E off A911

Burleigh Castle Solid, unostentatious 15th-century tower house, prominent in Scottish history; **farm** opposite provides key to bare and gloomy interior.

JUNCTION 8

9m (14.5km) E on A912

Falkland Palace
Formidable French-
Renaissance pile, the
most substantial
surviving relic of the
'Auld Alliance' between
Scotland and France;
embedded in the heart

of **Falkland,** a quaint
little township; royal
hunting seat and
summer palace of early
Stuart kings; carefully-
planned **gardens** have
herbaceous borders,
spring-flowering cherry,
autumnal maples,
gorgeous greenhouse
plants, colourful creeper
over old walls, a 'royal'
tennis court; altogether
a thoroughly
worthwhile attraction,
with atmospheric little
country-style shops
(coffee, antiques, meals)
round about.

4m (6.5km) E on B919
Burleigh Castle See
Junction 7

A912
Bridge of
Earn
Newburgh

2m(3.2km)
to J10

9

A912
Bridge of
Earn
Glenfarg
(B996)
Cupar (A913)

9m(14.4km)

N ↑

A91
St Andrews
Dundee
(A914)
Tay Bridge
Glenfarg
(B996)

8

No exit

2m(3.2km)
to J7

JUNCTION 9

*3m (5km) NE via Rhynd,
off A912*
Elcho Castle Old
fortified house of
architectural interest,
dreaming away the
centuries on bank of Tay
estuary; legends of
William Wallace the
Scottish patriot attached
to it.

ABERNETHY
4m (6.5km) E on A913
Sleepy village of
ecclesiastical memories
among water meadows
beside Tay and Earn
rivers; **round tower** is a
monkish survival from
11th century, very rare
in Scotland though
common in Ireland; near
church, a mysterious
Pictish **symbol stone;** in
mud at confluence of
the two rivers, optimists
fish for pearls.

*3m (5km) E at A912/A913
junction*
Bein Inn Delightful and
historic 'howff' among
Glenfarg woodlands;
agreeable service,
superior cuisine,
moderate prices. Tel:
(057 73) 216.

JUNCTION 10
2m (3km) N on A90
Perth See M85
Junction 1

3m (5km) NE via Perth on A85
Branklyn Garden See M85 Junction 1

JUNCTION 11

3m (5km) E on A9
Perth See M85 Junction 1

3m (5km) N and E on A85

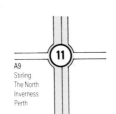

A9
Stirling
The North
Inverness
Perth

Huntingtower Castle

Grim stronghold with a grim history; young King James VI (afterwards James I of England) was kidnapped and held prisoner here.
Huntingtower restaurant, close to castle on A85, offers varied and interesting menu and is warmly recommended by locals; not expensive. Tel: (073 883) 241.

3m(4.8km)

6m (9.5km) NE on A9 and Atholl Street to A93

Scone Palace A castellated palace on 16th-century and earlier foundations, but chiefly of early 19th century; porcelain, furniture, clocks, needlework, family treasures of Earls of Mansfield. **Moot Hill** at Scone, legendary coronation place of Pictish kings, had notorious 'Stone of Scone' from 9th to 13th centuries (now in Westminster Abbey); well-timbered park and pinetum; coffee shop, restaurant, gift shop. Closed in winter. (This route to Scone Palace is not the shortest, but it avoids the extreme congestion of central Perth in summer months.)

M85
The N East
Dundee
Forfar
Aberdeen
A912
Perth

M85
Dundee
Forfar
Aberdeen
Braemar

2m(3.2km)
to J9